Happy Families

How to Make One ◆ How to Keep One

Happy Families

How to Make One ◆ *How to Keep One*

Bill Lucas

With clinical psychologist Dr Stephen Briers

B B C ACTIVE

Educational Publishers LLP trading as BBC Active
Edinburgh Gate
Harlow
Essex CM20 2JE
England

First published 2006

ISBN 0 563 51942 8

Commissioning editor: Emma Shackleton
Editor: Patricia Burgess
Text designer: Kevin O'Connor
Cover designer: Annette Peppis
Illustrator: Chris Long
Senior Production Controller: Man Fai Lau
Cover photograph by Hans Reinhard/Zeffa/Corbis

Printed and bound by Mateu Cromo, Spain

The Publisher's policy is to use paper manufactured from sustainable forests.

Dedication
Who else could it possibly be!

To my mother (and father, now dead) for being my first and most profound teachers.

To my sister Rachel – we've learnt so much about each other and about how to try to be happier and better parents in a complex world.

To my wife Henrietta, my life 'coach' and the person who inspires me to be creative and happy on a daily basis.

And to all of my three wonderful children – Tom, Bryony and Peter – from each of whom I learn so much.

Acknowledgements
Special thanks to my editor, Emma Shackleton, for believing in me in the first place and for introducing me to such a creative and talented collaborator, Stephen Briers.

The author would especially like to acknowledge the help of the Bristol Community Family Trust, whose model for stopping negative cycles is discussed on page 68.

Contents

Introduction

Someone dressed as Batman stands calmly on the battlements of Buckingham Palace to tell the world about the injustice felt by fathers who are denied access to their children. The whole of the children's care and education system in England is reorganized following the awful suffering and tragic death of Victoria Climbié. In 2003 the number of divorces granted in the UK was 166,700 – an increase of 3.7 per cent on the previous year. The UK currently has the highest rate of teenage pregnancy in Europe, with one in ten of all births being to teenage mothers. And even on a more light-hearted note, the world's most popular TV family – the Simpsons – has a father who is described by his wife Marge as someone who 'forgets birthdays, anniversaries, holidays (both religious and secular), chews with his mouth open, hangs out at a seedy bar with bums and lowlifes, blows his nose in towels and puts them back, and scratches himself with his keys'.

It would be easy to conclude that home life as we know it today is pretty grim, and that anyone choosing to write a book called *Happy Families: How to Make One, How to Keep One* must be either seriously deranged, ridiculously optimistic or deliberately ironic. I hope that by the time you have finished reading this book you will have concluded that I am none of these.

If there is any hint of irony intended, it is only in the choice of title, which may remind some people of just how much the family has evolved. If you have ever played the card game Happy Families, you may recall that the goal is to collect the four members of different nuclear families, each handily but anachronistically named after the profession of the male breadwinner: Mr Chalk, the Teacher, Mrs Chalk, the teacher's wife, Master Chalk, the teacher's son, and Miss Chalk, the teacher's daughter.

The world we live in today has moved a long way from this sort of family and is much more complicated. The nuclear family depicted in the card game still exists, but a contemporary set-up might also be a single parent and child, or include step-parents and children from different relationships all living under one roof.

Whatever set-up you live in, it's tough being a parent, but there are some practical things you can do to make sure that your family life is as happy as possible. The trouble is that the advice has become so specialized. There are books on babies, teenagers, divorce, step-children, sexuality, health, emotions...the list goes on and on. But the picture these volumes present is often a very fragmented one, and your bookshelves would be groaning under their weight if you bought even a fraction of them.

About this book

Happy Families tries to look holistically at one of the most dynamic, flexible and essential 'institutions' in the world today – the family. To do so, I have drawn on my own experiences of being a parent in a complex family, on the advice of my colleague Dr Stephen Briers, the clinical psychologist from BBC Television's *Little Angels* and *Teen Angels*, on the 'testimony' of many parents, children and young people, and on a wide range of research from many different disciplines.

Happy Families has eight chapters, each of which contains:

- An overview of what we know about the subject
- A set of questions about the topic
- A round-up of some of the key issues
- Five key principles that can be used to create your own unique version of a happy family, each with practical exercises for putting them into practice
- A troubleshooting section, giving clear advice and guidance on some of the difficult practical issues raised by each chapter.

If you glance at the contents page, you will see that some of the principles overlap. This is deliberate. While the context may be different in each chapter, there are some core principles, such as being positive and spending time on what matters, that are applicable in many different situations.

Of course, while there may be helpful principles, there is rarely one correct way of doing things. Consequently, any advice I give is offered in the spirit of being a fellow traveller and explorer. It represents one possible approach, not the *only* one. Indeed, as the modern family continues to develop, we are going into uncharted territory. We all need to work things out as we go along.

Changing with the times

While it's easy to focus on the negative aspects of the modern family, it's also worth noting that there have been changes for the better. For example, fathers now have a statutory right to paternity leave, and it's clearly possible to combine parenting with successful careers (look at Cherie and Tony Blair). Remember too, in the face of global and personal tragedies, the resilience and flexibility of the family, the power of its bonds and its adaptability to cultural and religious differences.

And don't forget that Homer Simpson, despite obvious failings, is a devoted if unconventional husband. The fact that the Simpsons stay together is partly what makes us want to watch the series. All our foibles are paraded in exaggerated form for us to see and laugh at, and the family soldiers on.

Given the extraordinary changes we are witnessing in so many areas of our life, such as technology, attitudes to marriage and the role of religion, there is a real sense in which the family remains the glue that holds the whole of society together. It was no accident that we saw the most generous international outpouring of support for the victims of the 2004 tsunami. A natural disaster had struck at the heart of family life across the world, indiscriminately destroying loved ones of all ages from many nations and leaving behind painful reminders of the fragility of families – orphaned children, distraught parents and grief-stricken grandparents.

The myth of a golden age

Read the newspapers today and you could be forgiven for thinking that the family is in terminal decline. Irresponsible parents are failing to instil the discipline of their forebears. Poverty is on the increase. Some 20 per cent of the population apparently do not have the basic numeracy and literacy skills to survive. Women are out working when they should be at home looking after their children. And there is a national outbreak of obesity that is the fault of parents.

This is quite wrong. It is a myth to think that it was all much better in times past. The discipline meted out then to children was often simply keeping the lid on problems that would surface painfully in later life. For much of the last century, poverty was more widespread than now and educational opportunity was only for the privileged few. Today the assumption is increasingly that you will be in full-time learning until you are eighteen, and that about half of school-leavers will continue in some kind of higher education. Women may still need to work outside the home, but in many cases they want to. They are consequently more fulfilled and more tired, just like their male partners. This is neither good nor bad, just different. It is how families manage their life that is the critical issue. And while it is true that we need to improve our diet dramatically, this is not the fault of families per se, although parents can play a really important role here.

The concept of happiness

A word about my interest in the idea of happiness. I am certainly not the first to have stressed the importance of it. Think of the founding fathers of America and their Declaration of Independence: 'We hold these truths to be self-evident, that all men are created equal, that they are endowed by their Creator with certain unalienable Rights, that among these are Life, Liberty and the pursuit of Happiness.' Neither will I be the last to emphasize it, for I see the pursuit of happiness as an integral part of modern family life. This means that I see love between couples, siblings, step-relatives and family friends, and across generations and cultures, as a goal of living. I believe that our inner life is just as important as our ability to change nappies or be a good step-parent.

And parenting, while sometimes an exhausting challenge, is one of the most rewarding opportunities we can seize with open arms if we are blessed with children.

CHAPTER 1 The Nature of Happiness

Happy families are all alike; every unhappy family is unhappy in its own way.

Leo Tolstoy, *Anna Karenina* (1873–7)

Have you ever consciously thought about your own happiness? Whether you have or not, perhaps you can take a moment to think about the following questions. Don't worry if you can't think of an answer to each one. You might find it helpful to chat about them with your partner.

- What makes you happy?
- What makes your partner (or closest friend) happy?
- What makes your children happy?
- Do you have a 'happiest day of your life' so far? If so, when was it?
- How happy are you now?
- Can you be happy if you have been divorced?
- Can step-children ever be really happy?
- Does happiness depend on material possessions?
- How much do you know about happiness?
- Can you be happy if one of your children is not happy?
- Can you be happy if your partner is not happy?
- How effectively does your family promote the happiness of all of its members?

Some people would say that if you have to start thinking consciously about happiness, you cannot be happy. But I am not so sure. For unless you are prepared to bring the idea of happiness more into your conscious mind (and thereafter, perhaps, into your unconscious), it may be that you will miss the opportunity to do things differently that could make you and your family feel happier.

Most people find it hard to say how happy they are at any one moment. For a start, our vocabulary is not subtle enough. While there are plenty of words to describe the extremes of happiness (joy, ecstasy, fulfilment) or unhappiness (misery, despair), there are few for those all-important in-between states. In the context of family life think of those moments when you have an inkling that something is not quite right, but cannot put your finger on it. Have you ever developed a gnawing uneasiness about something that has yet to surface so that you can grapple with it?

Perhaps you are reading this book because you are not enjoying family life at the moment and are looking for help to make you feel better about it. In this case, perhaps you will find comfort in what psychiatrist and author M. Scott Peck has to say: 'The truth is that our finest moments are most likely to occur when we are feeling deeply uncomfortable, unhappy, or unfulfilled. For it is only in such moments, propelled by our discomfort, that we are likely to step out of our ruts and start searching for different ways or truer answers.'

In other words, there is real value to being unhappy. At such times we tend to have the capacity to get our life into perspective. It is not just poets or songwriters who can extract meaning from feeling miserable; we all have this capacity. Perhaps it is helpful to see our unhappiness or dissatisfaction as a useful signal that something needs to change.

Douglas Adams has some interesting ideas about happiness in *The Hitch-hiker's Guide to the Galaxy* (1979). He describes some very intelligent robots created at an institute called MISPWOSO, who are given the capacity for happiness (or unhappiness). Their programers realize that they need to give the robots only three essential capacities: the capability to experience happiness or unhappiness; some situations or conditions in which these states can be created; and the ability to learn from experience.

On this basis, the more open robots are to change, the more likely they are to learn from experience. The more they learn from experience, the more likely they are to avoid those conditions that make them unhappy. And the full name of MISPWOSO, in case you have been wondering, is the Maximegalon Institute of Slowly and Painfully Working Out the Surprisingly Obvious. Perhaps it's as obvious as this for humans too.

In this chapter we will be examining some practical steps you can take to increase levels of happiness both for yourself and other members of your family.

What is happiness?

The card game Happy Families, to which the title of this book alludes, assumes that there is an association between happiness and family life. But it doesn't give us much insight into what a recipe for happiness might look like, or the ways in which families can effectively develop happiness among their members. And the media, with its emphasis on many of the superficial things in life, does not help much either.

In fact, research tells us that the ingredients for happiness are not necessarily the things that our culture and popular perception would lead us to believe are important. So, for example, financial prosperity (beyond a basic level) does not directly relate to life satisfaction. Even good health is barely related to happiness, often being taken for granted and only valued in its absence.

The things that *do* seem to have a bearing on happiness include having a stable relationship, a network of friends, a set of beliefs and a basic level of income. People who invest time in trying to work out what it means to be part of the world – in other words, what gives meaning to our existence – tend to be more fulfilled. Those who see that their life, in a sense, serves a higher purpose and has the potential for making a difference to society often seem to be happier. The same is true for those who consciously strive to make the world a better place and for those who have faith.

But the biggest contributors to happiness are features of our internal world and mental life. These specifically relate to the way we react to things that happen to us, our sense of our own identity, especially the degree to which we see ourselves as 'in control' of events. Throughout this book there will be plenty of opportunity to explore these contributors to happiness in more detail, which is good news. For while you may not be able to change your circumstances straight away, you can change the way you approach them.

Let me introduce you to an interesting theory that may help you to explain things that happen to you and how you feel about them. It's called the 'peak-end rule'. This rule says that our perception of how good or bad something has been is based on the average of two parts of our experience: how good or bad the peak of the experience was, and how good or bad the end was.

Let's say you have been on a family holiday and had awful weather for most of the time, but enjoyed sunny skies and sandy beaches for the last few days. In a situation like this, you might well look back and feel that you had a happy week overall. However, that same experience followed by a miserable journey home makes you more likely to see your time away as unhappy. Similarly, let's say that one of you is at home looking after the children. If the day starts with an argument, is then mostly enjoyable, but ends with a row just before your partner gets home, you are likely to view the day as an unhappy experience. Put simply, the most recent experience is what sticks in your mind and determines your mood.

Understanding the peak-end rule could help both you and your partner to be a little more understanding of each other. When it comes to being happy or unhappy, what has just happened to you assumes a special importance.

Luckily, the drive for happiness and self-fulfilment is essential to survival and growth. When something goes wrong, you pick yourself up and try again. Indeed, the degree to which you are open to change matters, as Douglas Adams was suggesting. While the major traumas of family life – divorce, separation and loss – all affect us negatively, most people adapt remarkably quickly. For example, research shows that children can be just as happy in loving and effective step-families as they are when they live with their biological parents.

In fact, the way you deal with the many lesser life challenges – for example, the amount of persistence you show – is just as likely to impact on your happiness. The most important thing to hang on to is that you can learn how to become happier. Contrary to Jane Austen's famous declaration in *Pride and Prejudice* (1813), 'Happiness in marriage is entirely a matter of chance', happiness is largely a matter of your mindset and the practical steps you are prepared to take to do things differently.

So if you are struggling to keep your eyes open as you read these words because your baby kept you up all night, or because you are working all hours to pay the bills, don't give up. Even if you are boiling with rage because your ex-partner has just done something that makes you want to explode, keep reading. For there are practical things you can do that will help you become happier in whatever type of family situation you currently find yourself. Let's explore some of these.

Five principles of happy family life

While there is no simple map to guide you through family life and ensure that the journey is a happy one, there are certain approaches that, if deliberately adopted, make it more likely that you will be happier for more of the time.

Principle 1: Be positive

Once upon a time, it was believed that who we are depended largely on the environment in which we grew up. So, for example, if you were raised in a poor neighbourhood, you were less likely to do well in life. Or if you were divorced, your children were bound to be damaged. This approach to life is called 'behaviourism'. Even though almost all behaviourist theories were based exclusively on experiments with animals, such as training dogs to salivate whenever a bell was rung, adherents held that all human actions were similarly determined by environment.

Another idea was that if fate were not to blame for an unhappy situation, it was somehow the fault of your genes. You will probably have heard the expression 'nature or nurture'. This suggests that things happen either because of what's in your gene pool (what you have inherited from your parents) or as result of things you learn along the way (what you learn from your parents and from living). Scientists argue fiercely about which of these two forces is the stronger one, but most agree that both are important.

In fact, we are neither the simple products of our environment nor the unalterable results of our parents' nature. It is more complex than this. And it is possible to change the way you behave very significantly. One of the most powerful elements in this is your mindset. It was psychologist Martin Seligman who first really challenged the establishment with his radical thinking about this during the 1990s. He came up with a concept that he called 'learned optimism'. This describes the positive mindset that successful people need to cultivate to help them achieve. Seligman suggests that the world is divided into two kinds of people: optimists and pessimists. It all comes down to the way you account for things that happen to you, your 'explanatory style'. Seligman describes this as having three elements: permanence, pervasiveness and personalization – the three Ps.

Have you ever wondered why people who seem to be similarly talented can have very different dispositions? Some are 'glass half-full' people, always seeing the positive side of things, while others are 'glass half-empty' types, always focusing on the negative. Some are knocked back for only a few moments when something goes wrong and rapidly evolve a way of seeing it as an isolated misfortune, while others immediately make it part of a pattern of failure and bad luck. The three Ps help to explain this.

Permanence: When something goes wrong, optimists see it as a one-off setback, while pessimists see it as something that always happens. A pessimist would say, 'Things like this always happen to me and the effects last for ever'.

Pervasiveness: When things go wrong, optimists realize it is because of a particular situation, but pessimists see it spreading right through their life. A pessimist would say, 'Things like this always happen to me and that's typical of everything I do in my life'.

Personalization: When things go wrong, optimists take control of events, while pessimists sink into a depression, imagining that the whole world is against them. A pessimist would say, 'Things like this always happen to me because I am unlucky/hopeless/stupid…'

Behaviourist theory suggests that you are a victim of your environment and situation. The concept of learned optimism and its associated techniques show that this need not be the case.

How optimistic are you?

Take a moment to think about your own life. Maybe you found yourself getting angry for the umpteenth time with your children because they seem incapable of sitting and behaving decently at supper.

▷ Did you find yourself feeling resigned to this state of affairs going on for ever? Or did you resolve to do something differently next time to ensure a happier mealtime? This is the 'permanence dimension'.

▷ Did your experience make you see mealtimes as part of a wider pattern of parenting in which your children are always naughty and you never seem to be able to do anything about it? Or did you stop to wonder what was causing the behaviour on this one occasion – perhaps you or your children were tired, for example – confident that it was just an isolated incident? This is the 'pervasiveness dimension'.

▷ And how personally did you take it? Did it make you feel bad that only you seem incapable of organizing a civilized mealtime when all your friends seem to get along just fine? Or were you able to be clear in your mind that there were good reasons why it all went wrong and that these were nothing to do with you, but rather because your children had an early start to their day, so were especially hungry. This is the 'personalization dimension'.

All three of these dimensions are united by one common strand: the need to be positive. While the concept of positive psychology may be relatively new, we have known about it for many years, as Martha Washington's often quoted remark of two centuries ago reminds us: 'The greatest part of our happiness or misery depends on our dispositions and not on our circumstances.'

American researcher Carol Dweck has gone further still, suggesting that some children become victim to an extreme version of the pessimistic mindset through being spoonfed at school or at home. She calls this 'learned helplessness', a condition in which the young person has come to depend so much on others that he or she has, in effect, become helpless to do things independently. You can find out more about how to encourage optimistic children who approach life with attitudes likely to foster happiness in Chapters 5 and 6.

Getting practical and positive

If you want to become more positive in your family life, you might like to follow these steps:

1. Look back on the previous week and make a note of all of the events that happened to you (for example, your children were late for school because you had an argument with your partner over breakfast).

2. Examine each event carefully. Using the three Ps, make up a statement to describe your explanation under each heading. Here are three examples using the case of the argument.

   Permanence: 'We must both be really tired at the moment to be so grumpy with each other. Let's try to have an early night.'

   Pervasiveness: 'It's a good thing that both of our jobs are going so well at the moment.'

   Personalization: 'Maybe I overreacted. I'll make a real effort to listen more carefully next time.'

3. If your statements are anything like the pessimistic examples on pages 9 and 10, reframe them so that you see the event as a one-off example of something that happened because of good reasons that were nothing to do with you and your life. For example, if you were late with the school run, your optimistic explanation could be: 'Oh dear, we all got a bit carried away at breakfast. I'll make a mental note not to start discussions about complex things at breakfast.'

4. You might like to notice how often an optimistic statement avoids the present tense (which implies things are fixed and stuck) and prefers to use the past tense (it's happened and over) along with the future tense (outlining something positive that you can do to put it right).

Principle 2: Be yourself

In Shakespeare's play *Hamlet*, its eponymous hero is given these words of advice by Polonius: 'This above all: to thine own self be true.' This is good advice for all parents to give to a child or, for that matter, to take themselves. Knowing who you are and being comfortable with this is at the heart of being happy and balanced as a member of a family. But how do you know who you are? Will the real you please step forward?

Parents find this whole area especially challenging given the large number of roles they play – carer, friend, provider and so forth (see Chapters 5 and 8 for more on this). Are you the same person when disciplining your child as the one who is making love to your partner or having to take a tough decision at work? The answer to this is 'yes', although it is often difficult to believe.

The psychologist Carl Jung (1875–1961) did a great deal of work on personality and how we think about ourselves. This in turn has led directly to the Myers-Briggs Type Indicator® (MBTI), a personality profiling system developed by Katherine Briggs and Isabel Briggs Myers. It is one of the most widely used and respected personality indicators in the world.

MBTI has four scales, each with two alternative perspectives denoted by a different letter in bold type. The sixteen combinations that result are ascribed to different personality types. No one combination is better than another; they are just different.

Source of energy > **E**xtravert or **I**ntrovert
Focus of attention > **S**ensor or i**N**tuitive
Way decisions are made > **T**hinker or **F**eeler
Attitude to world > **J**udger or **P**erceiver

Extravert: This type of person derives energy from outside himself, tends to be sociable, enjoys interaction, and often works things out as he goes along.

Introvert: This type of person derives energy from inside himself, tends to have a small number of deep relationships, reflects a lot and thinks carefully before speaking.

Sensor: This type of person gathers information in an exact and sequential manner, tending to be realistic, down-to-earth and specific.

Intuitive: This type gathers information in an imprecise, big-picture sort of way, relying on hunches, sense and generalizations that may not always be realistic.

Thinker: This type of person takes decisions in an impartial, fair-minded way, tending to be detached, logical and firm.

Feeler: This type of person takes decisions in a collaborative, interpersonal and subjective way. Such individuals place importance on people's feelings and are unwilling to cause upset if it can be avoided.

Judger: This type of person tends to have a controlled attitude to life, planning things with fixed deadlines.

Perceiver: This type's attitude towards life is likely to be 'wait and see', adaptable, flexible and open-ended.

According to Jung, personality is a combination of elements, so individuals tend to be described in terms of their principal characteristics. Here are some famous examples, reduced to four letters taken from the types described above. (Please note that these are just my own speculations.)

> Madonna – ESTP
> Margaret Thatcher – ENTJ
> Bill Clinton – ENFJ
> Elton John – ESFP
> Woody Allen – ISFJ
> Bill Gates – INTP

Can any type of person be happy? Yes. Are there aspects of personality that seem to lead to a greater likelihood of happiness in family life? We don't really know, although a number of researchers are exploring this area.

There seems to be an emerging consensus that some personality traits are likely to help people remain happy. Remaining positive, for example, is a good thing, and engaging actively in life is another. Being able to stick up for yourself and adopt moral or principled positions are also helpful, perhaps because they enable you to have a consistency of purpose that others might lack.

But at the heart of what it is to know yourself is the belief that you can develop, grow and become happier. Psychologist Abraham Maslow (1908–70) first came up with an idea that helps us to see this very clearly. He said that whatever the differences in individual temperament and personality, human beings have a hierarchy of needs, starting with basic things, such as water, food and sleep, moving up to being safe and loved, then to having enough self-esteem, and finally to what he called 'self-actualization'. Maslow's theory also suggests that we are motivated by unsatisfied needs. We all want to satisfy our needs and we can only do this by moving up the ladder.

For Maslow, self-actualization is the state of fulfilment in which the individual experiences himself to be functioning smoothly at the height of his powers. At these times – which Maslow calls 'peak experiences' – the person concerned is likely to feel most fully himself. A similar state to this has also been described by Mihalyi Csikszentmihalyi (pronounced 'cheek-sent-me-high') as the state of 'flow'. In such situations you are so engaged in what you are doing, and so intrinsically motivated by your enjoyment of it, that time seems to stop. This might come from reading a great book, playing an absorbing game, writing a diary, making love languorously – the choice is yours.

Maslow's views were a radical departure from the beliefs of previously influential psychologists, such as Sigmund Freud (1856–1939), who took a fairly pessimistic view of people, regarding them as animals dominated by their biological drive. Maslow recognized that although humans are essentially rational beings, they have a highly emotional response to the world. His hierarchy of needs looks like this:

SELF-ACTUALIZATION
ESTEEM NEEDS
BELONGING NEEDS
SAFETY NEEDS
PHYSIOLOGICAL NEEDS

This diagram helps us to understand that we are unlikely to be motivated to pursue higher forms of happiness unless many of our lower-level needs have been satisfied. If you are hungry or miserable, for example, doing something to develop yourself may not be on your agenda. Most people find this theory a convincing and helpful one, although it must be noted that it is possible to do things even when few of our needs are being satisfied and we are really desperate – something many hard-pressed parents know to be true.

Consequently, if there is no space in your life at present to think about your own individual needs, you are likely to be feeling frustrated. The creative thinking guru Edward de Bono puts it like this: 'Unhappiness is best defined as the difference between our talents and our expectations.' If you want something for yourself that is too far out of your grasp, you are likely to feel unsatisfied.

Another real advantage to developing yourself is that the more you explore your own talents, the more you are likely to become an all-round developed person. If you can do this effectively, you stop being defined by just one aspect of your personality or experience – 'He works long hours'; 'She's a great mum'; 'He's a terrific stepdad'. Instead, people begin to see you as a more complex person, caring for your children, being part of a church choir and taking up long-distance running, for example. The practical benefits of this are huge, for it allows you to go through a bad patch in one area of your life while leaving other areas unimpaired. Of course, managing the transition between the roles that these different areas require is not always easy.

Traditionally, the family has been a very good vehicle for meeting the basic physical and emotional needs of its members: indeed, the institution appears to have evolved precisely because of that. However, one of the greatest challenges for the modern family is how it can help its members to meet some of their higher-level needs for actualization.

Ironically, Maslow argues that as individuals become more self-actualizing, they tend to move away from their identification with groups to become more uniquely individual. During adolescence, children will often actively disengage from their family in order to develop an identity that feels more authentic to them (even if this involves finding some new group to identify with as they struggle to find out who they really are). Families that wish to foster self-actualization will therefore need to be especially flexible and innovative if they are to cater for the growth needs of their members.

Help growth and self-discovery

1. Encourage each other to explore talents, interests and activities that will open up new horizons.

2. Make and protect space for family members to 'do their own thing', as well as organizing joint activities that the family can enjoy together.

3. Support the development of relationships and contacts outside the family. Such relationships will allow members to experience themselves in different ways and to enjoy the growth opportunities provided through contact with a more diverse range of people.

4. Show an interest in and celebrate the self-exploration of family members: this might include attending your five-year-old's first 'art exhibition' (six of her paintings stuck up on her bedroom wall) or keeping your opinions firmly to yourself when your teenager arrives at the breakfast table wearing clothes you wouldn't be seen dead in.

Do you really know yourself?

How much do you know about the real you? If you are interested in finding out more, you could:

▷ Read up about the Myers-Briggs Type Indicator®. The website www.humanetrics.com allows you to find out your personality type online. Or log on to www.authentichappiness.org, a website created by Martin Seligman, which provides a number of similar but possibly more accessible approaches to establishing your individual characteristics, including your 'signature strengths'.

▷ Ask your partner to tell you what he or she really likes about your personality (and, if you are brave, what they like less).

▷ Agree with your partner (and possibly with your children if they are old enough to understand) that once a week you are going to take some time to yourself. Explain that this is something each member of the family can do. Call it 'Mum's time' or 'Dad's time', and be really strict about taking it. It need only be half an hour to read a book if your life is really full on and demanding, but it will give you a vital breathing space.

▷ Make a mid-year resolution to try learning something new, or to take up an activity that you have never tried before.

Principle 3: Be open to change

Stop and think for a moment about how many things to do with the family have changed over the last fifty years. This is a good topic of conversation with parents and grandparents, and most people find it easy to come up with a long list. Indeed, almost the only thing that has remained constant is the fact that however a family is organized and whatever its membership, it is a powerful set of relationships.

It was the scientist Charles Darwin (1809–82) who first pointed out a simple truth about change: 'It is not the strongest of the species that survive, nor the most intelligent, but the ones most responsive to change.'

While Darwin may have been looking at wild creatures on a remote island, many families bear more than a passing resemblance to this description. But in terms of being happy, it's more than mere evolution. People who adapt survive. People who are open to change thrive.

Researchers Robert Crosnoe and Glen Elder have a gone a stage further. They have recently shown that 'an openness to change in both family life and work life is associated with a 23 per cent greater likelihood of maintaining high levels of life satisfaction'.

Of course, it is easy to tell someone that they will feel happier if they are open to change. In practice, it is much more difficult to do this when the change facing you is unwanted and unexpected. Perhaps your partner walks out on you; a close relative falls seriously ill; your child becomes depressed.

Nevertheless, there are some approaches to managing changes – even apparently undesirable ones – that seem to increase your chances of turning them to your advantage.

How to deal with change

Are you open to change? Or do you find yourself tensing up and becoming defensive whenever you are asked to do something different? Next time you are faced with change in your family, try some of these approaches to help you.

Notice what has and hasn't changed. Studies of depressed people have consistently demonstrated the presence of a bias in their thinking, known as 'catastrophizing'. This is a tendency not only to assume the worst in any given situation, but also to allow one mishap to develop into a series of misfortunes. For example: 'I have just got a parking ticket. What if paying the fine means I struggle to pay the mortgage this month? If our financial circumstances get worse, the house could be repossessed. We could all end up on the street...' If you have a tendency towards this kind of thinking, it may be necessary to take a cool, calm look at the situation and take stock realistically.

Carefully describe to yourself the change you are experiencing. What are you feeling in response? Talk openly about it. (Most people experience a range of negative emotions, including anger and denial, until the moment comes when they feel able at least to experiment with the new situation.)

Write down the change that's worrying you. Simply putting a name to a worry can help; it will also force you to be specific.

Think what would be the worst thing that the change could bring. It might not be as bad as you fear.

Consider how the change might improve your life. Perhaps you have looked only at the negative side so far.

Remember the times when you have dealt with something like this before. Make a list of all the things that might help you in your current situation.

Ask for the opinions and advice of your family and friends. You could consider what you might say to someone if they came to you with a similar problem.

Make a list of all the positive ways ahead you can think of. Choose the one(s) that seem most likely to work. Then, rather than trying to get your head round the whole situation, just make sure you do one thing, however small, that will move you forward. As the old proverb has it, a journey of a thousand miles does indeed begin with a single step, and focusing on small, manageable goals is often the best way to deal with situations that can otherwise feel overwhelming.

The more you are able to deal with change effectively, the more likely you are to be open to it. Once you have accumulated several examples of responding positively to change in ways that you feel good about, this will help build your confidence in your ability to adapt and manage future challenges.

There are some other things that help too.

Be 'mindful' and learn to live in the moment

The world is changing so rapidly that it is becoming even more important to enjoy the moment. Originally a Buddhist concept, the idea of living in the present (rather than dwelling in the past or fretting about the future) is especially important when we are all so busy and stressed. Sometimes called 'mindfulness', it can be summarized as follows.

If you are too busy to enjoy the here and now of what you are doing, you have probably got your life dangerously out of kilter. Your own well-being will be greatly enhanced if you make sure that you enjoy the moment. Otherwise your child may take her first steps when you are too busy to notice. Or you might spend a family day out attached to your mobile phone and not really taking part at all.

Martin Seligman tells the story of a novice monk who arrives before his teacher after a three-year course of study to face strenuous inquisition on the deep mysteries of his faith. The teacher has only one question for him: 'In the doorway were the flowers to the right or the left of the umbrella?' Unable to answer, the student leaves dejectedly for another three years of study. (Had he been mindful, he would have known the answer.)

At a deeper level, it is sometimes important just to 'be', to enjoy things without having to analyse why you are enjoying them. The poet John

Keats (1795–1821) had a phrase for this – 'negative capability'. This is 'when man is capable of being in uncertainties, mysteries, doubts, without any irritable reaching after fact and reason'. As Keats says in his 'Ode to a Nightingale':

> *It is a flaw*
> *In happiness to see beyond our bourn.*
> *It forces the summer skies to mourn*
> *It spoils the singing of the nightingale.*

Enjoy the moment. Be open to change. And be ready to move on. For this is what Darwin means by 'responsive to change'. If you are open to change, not only do you have a mindset that makes you better able to deal with it, but you are also likely to be able to adapt and learn from your experiences.

Principle 4: Make friends

We all need to belong. Look back at Maslow's hierarchy on page 14. Unless we feel that we belong, we tend to feel lonely, isolated and ultimately worthless.

The phenomenal success of the website Friends Reunited is a dramatic testimony to this most human of needs. We make firm friends at school and then all go our separate ways, but we remain curious about the progress of our friends. Did Guy and Kate get married? Where's Bill living these days? I wonder if Helen ever had children? Did Chris ever come out and tell his parents he is gay? And so on.

Another indicator of the importance of friends is the practice of networking in the business environment. When it comes to getting business or finding your next job, it seems that you are more likely to be successful if you have cultivated a network of friends and contacts who think well enough of you to offer help when you need it. This is not a new idea. During the 1960s sociologist Stanley Milgram popularized the phrase 'six degrees of separation'. This is also known as the 'small world phenomenon' – the idea that we are all connected to each other by a chain of (at most) six people. This might not always be true, but it is amazing how often, if you put your mind to it, you can think of someone who knows someone who knows the person you need to talk to.

Friends are particularly important these days as they often provide continuity to family units that continually restructure and update themselves. The geographical dispersal of families means that a local network of friends can often fulfil many of the functions formerly provided by relatives – helping a woman cope with post-natal depression, for example, and offering practical advice and support to new parents. A circle of friends can provide babysitters, dog-walkers and lift-givers. They can help you to check out important family facts – the going rate for pocket money, what's acceptable at a sleepover, how to talk about sex with your child. It's not just quiz show contestants who sometimes need to 'phone a friend'.

People who think about the way society is organized have long noticed that bonds of friendship are the 'glue' that hold communities together. According to political scientist Robert Putnam, this is something called 'social capital' (as opposed to financial capital): 'Social capital refers to connections among individuals – social networks and the norms of reciprocity and trustworthiness that arise from them.' In other words, friendship has a real value.

Look back at the information about personality types on page 12. If you are naturally extraverted, you are, according to researcher Richard Wiseman, not only likely to be happier, but also luckier. He found that extraverted people are significantly more likely to make their own luck by talking with their circle of friends. 'The more people they meet, the greater opportunity they have of running into someone who has a positive effect on their lives.'

Making friends

There have been times in my life when I have felt that I do not have enough friends. As a teenager, I remember envying my friends who seemed to know lots of girls. Then, when I went on to university, there were some painful moments as I realized I was going to have to start again almost from scratch. Later in life, house and job moves produced similar anxiety. At such times you become consciously aware of what is involved in the making of friends. Then, as you become a parent, you make friends through association with playgroups, schools, clubs and sports teams.

What's your social capital?

▷ Stop for a moment and take stock of your own 'social capital'. How many people do you count as your really good friends – those with whom you can talk about the most difficult issues in life?

How to make friends

Let's assume that you are starting again from scratch. What on earth do you do?

1. Start by acknowledging any fears you may have about this subject. For, depending on your personality and the circumstances you find yourself in, making friends can be intimidating. You are likely to have to make the first approach, and there is always the lurking fear that you may be rejected.

2. Remember where you met the good friends that you've had in your life. See what this suggests to you that might work now.

3. Go to community activities, such as sporting events, concerts, readings, special interest groups and local meetings. Enrol on a course or join a church or other faith group. If money is tight, use your local library to look in the newspaper for information about free events.

4. Become a volunteer for a charity, or offer to help at a local school.

5. Have you ever noticed how dog-walkers often stop and chat? If you like dogs, get one and go for walks.

6. If you feel confident enough, use an Internet chat room.

7. Practise some opening lines that work for you.

8. Once you have established contact with someone who seems interesting, suggest that you meet up for a coffee or go for a walk together.

It is probably helpful to have a number of different ways of consciously trying to make friends and, if you find this difficult, to keep trying different ones until you feel comfortable.

Modern families are more flexible than ever before, and this creates more possibilities for friendship. Of course, it can also add its own strain because human beings still need to be private as well as surrounded by people – autonomous as well as gregarious. But provided that you can build in opportunities for the quieter, more reflective moments that we all need, you can strike a balance.

Principle 5: Take control

The notion of empowerment has firmly taken hold in these more egalitarian times, but it's important to choose your battles carefully – an idea expressed most succinctly nearly 800 years ago.

Happy Families

God grant me the serenity to accept the things I cannot change;
Courage to change the things I can;
And wisdom to know the difference.

St Francis of Assisi (1181–1226)

About fifty years ago the psychologist Julian Rotter came up with a theory about the way we view what happens to us. He called it the 'locus of control'. Those who have an internal locus of control believe that they can influence events by what they do. They might, for example, believe they can become better parents or happier with life by working at it. Those with an external locus of control are more likely to account for things by attributing them to outside factors, such as the weather, a recent house move or a new job.

So how do you end up with an internal rather than an external locus of control? People who have an internal locus of control feel motivated from within and more in control of their lives. The general consensus among researchers is that if your parents were very controlling – 'authoritarian' is the word sometimes used ('Get outside and get on with your football practice') – you are likely to grow up with an external locus of control. If your parents were kinder and encouraged you to see the benefits of your actions ('If you practise kicking the ball, you are likely to get better at scoring goals'), you would be likelier to have an internal locus of control. Very stressful life events, especially at an early age, can also have the effect of making you more likely to have an external locus of control.

The more you get your life in control, the happier you are likely to be. And being in control also often means that you stop trying to change the things over which have little influence.

If you are reading this in the midst of the mayhem that passes for family life in my home from time to time, you might find the idea of being in control an impossibly outrageous one. But don't give up. Even if you are little more than a novice 'air-traffic controller', ensuring that there are not too many 'in-flight collisions' in your living room, you are making progress.

Control, in the sense I have been describing it, is helpful, but not for its own sake. For being in control begs the question, control of what? Consequently, any recognition of the importance of taking more internal control needs to be accompanied by the setting of achievable goals for yourself. Goals are essential if you want to achieve control. You will be more likely to make better use of your time and more likely to have the right mindset to achieve the goals.

One of the many interesting things about the way your brain works is that when you focus on something, it notices and starts to process related information, exploring things that might be of interest to you and finding connections with your interests. A simple example of this is when you buy a new car, you suddenly start noticing other cars of the same make because your brain is tuned into this.

Can goals help to control your life?

Try these simple steps to work out your current goals. You could do it as an individual exercise, work with your partner, or even talk it through as a whole family.

▶ The all-important first step is to work out what your goals are (for more help with this, see Chapter 8). It might help to think about different areas of your life to ensure that you cast your net widely. Perhaps the chapter headings of this book could give you some ideas. Make a note of everything you come up with.

▶ Once you have some clear ideas, you need to work out which are the most important goals in your personal circumstances. For example, if you have a very young family, your goal might be the modest one of having a civilized adult supper once a month with your partner. Or if you are having difficulties with your children's behaviour, you might want just to focus on making the weekly trip to the supermarket a less stressful experience. Of if your ex-partner is being difficult, it might be appropriate to steel yourself for a meeting to try to sort things out.

▶ Choose no more than three goals at any one time. Too many goals and you are unlikely to be able to achieve them. Be precise and realistic. Don't aim too high, but equally don't aim too low. Set a timescale. And write your goals down. This simple act will help you to become committed to them.

▶ Finally, share some of your goals with a small number of people you can trust. This way they stop being just your private property and start attracting the supportive interest of others. A good example of this is the way in which friends can encourage you to stop smoking if they know this is what you want. Or perhaps you are having difficulty in managing your anger at home; the slightest thing drives you into an unnecessary rage. If the family knows that you are trying to do something about it, they can help you and even congratulate you as they notice a change in your behaviour.

People who set goals and take internal responsibility for their life tend to find that they spend more time on the things that matter and take action to avoid things that cause them unhappiness. As golfer Gary Player is reputed to have said, 'The harder you work, the luckier you get'.

A recipe for happiness

Let's close this chapter with some questions for you to ponder. What's the recipe for happiness in your family? How much do you know about the ingredients that make for happiness in those closest to you? Before you read on, are you able to articulate what seems to make you and yours happy? Stop and think for a moment, then fill in the chart below.

Things that make you feel good	Things that make you feel bad	Things that you would like to change

Troubleshooting

A book cannot possibly deal with your individual situation and specific concerns. But here (and at the end of every chapter) are a few suggestions for dealing with some of the problems you may have. Please take them in the spirit in which they are offered: as signposts for possible action rather than definitive instructions.

No amount of positive thinking seems to stop me feeling depressed.

Thoughts, feelings and actions all influence each other. Sometimes seeking to change your behaviour rather than your thinking can result in positive experiences that start to make you feel better. Depressed people tend to be passive and feel very helpless.

The question to ask yourself is: 'If I weren't feeling so down, what sort of things might I be doing?' Then choose a couple of these things and systematically set out to do them – even if you don't feel like it at first.

If your efforts to modify your behaviour and your thinking still have no effect on your mood, your depression could be serious and the time has come to seek help from your GP.

I don't like myself.

This is a real case of chicken and egg. Depressed people tend to think in a biased and distorted way about themselves, the world and the future: this is part and parcel of the way depression impacts on your thinking.

The chances are that if you are already feeling down, you will be much more receptive to 'evidence' suggesting you are a rotten or useless person, and pay no attention at all to information that would contradict your negative assumptions.

Nobody is completely bad, so rather than thinking in such all-consuming terms, ask yourself whether there are aspects of yourself that you or other people do like or admire. Better still, ask your family and friends what they see in you. Make a list of your strengths and see whether you can identify experiences or relationships that keep your negative self-image intact. If you draw a blank, maybe it would be helpful to explore some of these issues with a counsellor or psychologist.

I find change very threatening.

Change is threatening, but it is also unavoidable. Don't forget that it can be exciting too and is a necessary condition for our growth as people. Look closely at the pros and cons of any change you are considering: how might it benefit you, and how might it disadvantage you? Hang on to the potential advantages it could bring.

Try not to lose sight of the bigger picture. Is the change you are contemplating that big a deal in the great scheme of things? What is the worst that can happen? Will you have regrets at the end of your life if you leave things as they are?

As with all anxieties, fear of change is something that can be managed much more easily if you talk it through with someone else. This enables you to view the situation from another person's perspective and keep things in proportion. Susan Jeffers' book *Feel the Fear and Do It Anyway* (1997) is a very helpful read for anyone struggling with this issue.

I can't seem to make friends.

Probably the best thing you can do is to take up some interest or hobby that brings you into regular contact with people who like the same sort of things you do. This takes the pressure off and means that you will automatically have something to talk about. If you are feeling brave, you can check out with people you trust whether there is anything you are doing that might be off-putting to others.

Anxiety in social situations sometimes leads people to develop strategies (such as avoiding eye contact) that actually make things worse. Training courses in social skills are widely available if there are habits you need to break, or you just need to develop more confidence around other people.

Nothing I can do will make me happy.

This is the voice of clinical depression speaking. Have you really tried everything or is the belief itself keeping you stuck? There are a lot of formerly miserable people out there who now know different, but you have to be prepared to take the first step towards seeking help.

A good GP will be able to advise you about a range of options you might consider. If you really think like this, admit you have a problem and make an appointment. What have you got to lose?

Moving on

In this chapter we have begun to explore something of what it is to be happy. Now let's move on to one more general chapter, this time on the essential cornerstone of all families – effective communication.

As actor John Barrymore (1882–1942) once remarked, 'Happiness sneaks through a door you didn't know that you left open.' Keep that door ajar and read on.

CHAPTER 2 Communication that Works

INSPECTOR CLOUSEAU: *(to hotel receptionist)* Does your dog bite?

RECEPTIONIST: No.

CLOUSEAU: *(to the dog)* Nice doggie.

(Dog bites Clouseau.)

CLOUSEAU: I thought you said it didn't bite.

RECEPTIONIST: That's not my dog.

The Pink Panther (1964)

Have you ever consciously thought about how well you communicate with each other in your family? Try the following questions to get you going. You might find it helpful to chat about them with your partner.

- How often do you communicate with other members of your family?
- Which methods work best for you?
- How open are you with other members of your family?
- How much do you know about how those close to you like to communicate?
- What do you find most difficult to talk about?
- How good a listener are you?
- What's the best way to make yourself understood within your family?
- What gets in the way of your understanding others?
- What are the obstacles to effective communication?
- Is there a difference between talking and communicating?
- Can you change your communication style according to the circumstances?

In the previous chapter you found out about the ways in which you can take more control of your life and become happier. In this chapter you can explore some of the ways in which you can avoid the kind of situation in which Inspector Clouseau (and all of us from time to time) find ourselves.

Over the last few decades there has been an extraordinary technological revolution in the way we communicate. We can follow the efforts of solo round-the-world yachtswoman Ellen MacArthur on a website that shows live digital images of her clinging to the mast as she repairs it, with the sea churning below. Children can indulge in a horrific craze for bullying each other, filming it on their mobile phones, and then texting the images to their friends. Misguided e-mails about 'burying bad news' amidst the turmoil of 9/11, or details of a sexual tryst, can lead to resignations or even dismissal.

Where once the family telephone was monopolized by teenagers, it is now likely to lie idle while they talk to their friends on the latest generation of mobiles or in computer chat rooms. That's when they're not surfing the net or playing online games.

Effective communication

Despite amazing technological advances, the basic principles for effective communication remain the same. You need to work at it, be honest, be respectful and, above all, make time for it in the crowded world of family life.

It's certainly worth becoming better at communication because the evidence we have all points to a very close link between open communication and secure relationships. In other words, if you are an effective, open communicator, you are likely to have better relationships with your family members. The harsh reality is that poor communication is strongly associated with marital breakdown and behavioural problems in children.

Some families seem particularly good at communication: talking, listening, hugging and helping go on without anyone really being aware. For other people, it seems harder. Grumpy remarks, critical comments, misunderstandings and much unhappiness seem to be the norm.

As with so much in family life, it is very easy to assume that the current situation, however unsatisfactory, is likely to continue and cannot be much improved. This is quite wrong. However poor the state of communication in your family home, it can improve, so take heart.

It is possible to learn how to be assertive within a family, both as a parent and as a child, without losing your cool. There are ways of speaking that are more likely to work than others and that can be practised. And you can even choose to make the whole issue of communication something that you explore together as a family.

Often what is not said is as important as what is. A sullen gesture, a slammed door, a long pause – all these actions can speak much louder than words.

Above all, the way you communicate as an adult will set the tone for everyone else. If you mean what you say and do what you say, then all is likely to be well. By contrast, if there is a mismatch between what you say you believe and what you actually do, it is your actions that most of the family are likely to follow.

Given that we all make mistakes in family life, it is particularly heartening to know that where there is genuine communication taking place in a family, it is much more likely that the mistakes you and others make will be forgiven and forgotten.

Five principles of effective communication

Of course, what's written above is easy to say, but much harder to do. So let's get real by seeing how principles can be turned into actions.

Principle 1: Be open

There was a time when children were meant to be seen and not heard. And there was another time when many husbands and wives shared only a small part of their life with each other. Communication in such homes must have been stilted, limited and frustrating.

In today's complex families, which may have 'absent' fathers or mothers, such a view of communication simply does not hold. It would even be mildly ridiculous in the age of the mobile phone. Now that we are able to see the intimate details of a family disagreement in a soap opera such as *EastEnders*, or peer inside people's glamorized lives in *Hello!* magazine, ideas of what constitutes a happy and fulfilled home life are necessarily going to be much higher.

Have you ever caught yourself asking your partner or child how their day was and then not really listening to the answer? Or taking a decision about a family holiday without really discussing the options and considering the needs of different family members? Most of us have. In both cases, we are not being truly open in our communication. In the first example we closed our ears, and in the second we withheld vital information.

Sometimes we are not open in other ways. A child asks you if she can watch a certain film and you give an answer that is vague. Perhaps you say

29

'probably'. Or possibly you say 'yes', knowing that it will not be practical. Or maybe you simply grunt in such a way that your child doesn't know whether you are agreeing or disagreeing with the request. Of course, the film tends to be watched whatever your wishes. In fact, this last tactic is often a way in which parents deliberately (or unconsciously) avoid having to confront the real issue (is the film appropriate for the age of the child?) by giving a non-answer. All these examples illustrate communication that is not open.

Open communication is direct, respectful and timely within a positive atmosphere. Throughout *Happy Families* you will find examples of how it applies to every aspect of family life, and in the next chapter we will explore its key role in the development of relationships.

For now, it's enough to know that there are three simple ways to promote openness...

Watch your tone

Everyone knows that tone matters, so try this subtle shift. Every time you want someone to do something, instead of telling them to do it, suggest that they 'might like to' do it. 'Get on with your homework now' becomes 'You might like to start your homework now or you won't have finished before the start of that programme you want to watch'.

See how many examples there are in a typical day when you tell others around you what to do rather than leaving them to work it out for themselves. If you use the phrase 'might like to', it leaves people space to think and act for themselves. They might like 'not to'. Or they might have a better idea to try out. Either way, they are in control.

Write things down sometimes

Obviously, much of the essential communication in a family never ends up on paper. It is spoken, often as people are rushing around the house or getting ready to go out. But sometimes notes, messages and letters can be useful additions.

A note can:
- Give instructions
- Act as a reminder
- Be a thank you
- Remind someone that you are thinking about them.

A message can:
- Show someone you are thinking about their needs
- Relay communication from someone else.

A letter can:

- Be a great way of telling someone that you love them (as well as all the other ways)
- Be a means of sharing complicated information
- Give a member of your family time to process what you are thinking
- Say sorry for something (but this is no substitute for an immediate face-to-face apology).

The written word is not an alternative to speaking, hugging and other demonstrations of affection. But with so much 'noise' around, it pays to be creative in the ways you communicate.

Spot your hidden conversations

Have you ever had moments like this?

> DAD WALKS INTO A ROOM WHERE HIS TEENAGE DAUGHTER IS WATCHING THE TV.
>
> **Dad**: Now that you've got SATs coming up, I really want you to spend more time on your homework. [*Thinks: You're watching too much TV, so it's always far too late when you start doing your school work and I am finding this really irritating.*]
>
> **Daughter**: Sure. [*Thinks: Homework's boring. None of my friends is doing much at the moment. Why don't you get off my back?*]
>
> **Dad**: So can you turn the TV off and get started? [*Thinks: That's better. Now I'm really laying it on the line.*]
>
> **Daughter**: But it's just started. I'll turn it off in fifty minutes. [*Thinks: I thought we were talking about homework. Dad will give up if I just keep my head down. Then he'll leave me in peace.*]
>
> **Dad**: I told you to turn off the TV. [*Thinks: Why doesn't she take any notice of what I say?*]
>
> DAD STOMPS OFF.
>
> **Daughter**: Sure. [*Thinks: It worked! And by tomorrow he'll have forgotten about the homework with a bit of luck.*]

In this case, the father is grappling with more than homework and school tests. He is angry about his inability to establish clearer rules about watching the television, and he got the principle (of how much time his daughter should generally be spending doing her homework) muddled up with the practicality (of what she was doing at the moment of their conversation). It's also not a good idea to talk to someone who is watching the television, as they are able to give you only a small part of their attention.

The bracketed thoughts represent what lies hidden below the surface in so many family conversations. If you don't believe me, listen out for them in your home. Draw two columns on a sheet of paper as shown below and note down what is said and what you think the underlying thoughts and feeling are. This can be done either immediately or later, depending on whether you are directly involved in the conversation.

Words spoken	What was really being said (i.e. thought and felt)

Sometimes the hidden communication is so powerful that it effectively creates a parallel universe in which a different set of 'rules' operates. These unspoken rules often involve things such as:

- The power of adults (Adults are always right in this house.)
- The power of children (Children pretty much do what they want in this house.)
- Topics of conversation (We don't talk about sex, death, illness or a particular family member, often an absent parent.)
- The role of emotions (It's wrong to be angry and we don't like to talk about feelings.)
- Mealtimes (These don't really exist as we never sit down to eat as a family.)

In some homes these unwritten and unspoken rules sit alongside the things that everybody is open about. So, for example, it is perfectly possible that a parent might suggest a discussion about something with a child, when the child knows only too well that, as the parent is 'always right', real discussion is fairly futile. Or it might be that a parent is open about not wanting their children to use bad language, but closed to talking frankly about matters such as contraception and sexuality.

What are your unspoken rules?

Think about things in your own home. Are there any unspoken rules? If so, what impact are they having on your family life?

How to be more open in your communication

1. Look for the positive. Praise those around you many times more than you blame them. This is almost bound to challenge any hidden rules and ensure that the environment is right for open communication.

2. Don't assume that your family knows you so well that you don't have to work at communicating with them.

3. Stop and think about how your position as an adult in the family gives you extra power. This does not mean that you have to stop taking responsibility as a parent. Indeed, when challenged by children as to why they should do what you say, it may spur you on to resort to the age-old refrain, 'Because I say so,' with a determined expression on your face. On the contrary, it might suggest that there is little point in pretending there is an open agenda as you start a conversation about all the things that parents have to deal with (bedtimes, sleepovers, homework, undesirable friends and so forth).

4. Check what is really going on. When you think what is being said masks quite different thoughts, find out if you are right. You could gently ask whether what you think you have heard is an accurate description of what is being said. (See more about how you can do this without causing mayhem on page 37.)

5. Use humour. The great thing about this, even if your sense of humour is terrible and provokes embarrassment in your family, is that it forces people to look for other meanings in what is being communicated. This in turn makes it less likely that things better open remain hidden.

Principle 2: Be true to what you say

Why do we stop trusting some politicians? Why do some managers get a reputation for being unreliable? And why do some children and adults appear to take so little notice of what others say?

The answers to all these questions are often to do with a mismatch between what people say and what they actually do. It was US psychologist Chris Argyris who first developed a theory to explain this. He suggested that we all have a mental map as to how we and others behave in certain situations. We also develop ways of talking about what we believe. Argyris pointed out that what we say we believe and what we actually do are often very different things. He calls the things we do our 'theory in use' and the things we say our 'espoused theory'. He suggests that it is common for individuals to say one thing and do another, and that if the gap between what people say and do gets too big, this can be very difficult for those around them. It tends to lead to a lack of trust and, in some cases, outright scorn or derision.

For example, if you say that you believe in allowing your child to develop her own view of the world but spend your whole time telling her what to think, this might be problematic. Similarly, in the workplace environment you might cut meetings short by saying that an emergency has arisen, but the truth could be that you are just impatient and see your time as more valuable than other people's.

If you are trying to be open in your communication, it is important to avoid hidden or confusing messages, especially in the form of discrepancies between what you say and how you say it. There is little value in praise delivered in a flat, uninterested tone of voice. Conversely, studies show that children's suspicions are readily aroused if they feel praise is artificially effusive and not related to an honest description of their efforts.

With children, be aware that what you communicate through your actions is just as important, if not more so, as what you say with words. For example, it is no good telling a child it is wrong to hit if you use smacking as a means of discipline. When non-verbal signals are at odds with what you say, people tend to become confused and uncertain. They look for other information to resolve the discrepancy, and finally, if unsuccessful, tend to react negatively, getting angry or withdrawing altogether.

Another aspect of being true to what you say is recognizing that the more you can concentrate on what you are feeling (rather than speculating about other family members), the better. You are likely to be more effective in your communication if you focus on really 'owning' your feelings and reactions.

If you are having a conversation – especially a sensitive one – try to concentrate on statements about yourself and your feelings rather than comments that appear to be about the other person or his actions. Try using 'I' rather than 'you'. If you can keep the focus on your reactions to specific incidents or issues rather than making generalized remarks about the other person, you are much less likely to arouse antagonism.

There is a world of difference between saying 'You are so unreliable' and 'I felt let down and irritated when you turned up thirty minutes after the time we had agreed'. The first is a judgement on the person and is likely to produce a defensive or retaliatory response. The second is a comment about your experience that the other person is in no position to challenge and that is more likely to take the conversation forward.

Do your words match your actions?

Look at the following list of issues, and add any others you like. For each one, see if you can work out what you tend to do (your theory in use) and what you say you do (your espoused theory). Ideally, you will be putting the same thing in each column. If you are uncertain what to put in the right-hand column, ask your partner or a close friend to help you.

The issue	What you say	What you do
Being reliable		
Being truthful		
Being open and involving others		
Listening		
Keeping to time		
Working at weekends		
Doing the housework		

Principle 3: Listen, ask and check that you've been heard

Ever feel that people don't listen to you? Ever find that, despite having told everyone in your family that you are going to be away for a few days, you are confronted with blank faces when you ask a simple question about who is going to do something in your stead? Of course you do. We all do. As Albert Einstein (1879–1955) once said: 'The major problem in communication is the illusion that it has happened.'

In modern family life there is an awful lot of noise and we are all very busy. At home, and in most workplaces, you must take particular care to ensure that you listen well and that, when you are in communication mode, those around you are actually willing and able to hear what you are trying to say.

If you have ever listened to the Simon and Garfunkel song 'The Sound of Silence', you'll recognize the following words:

> *And in the naked light I saw*
> *Ten thousand people, maybe more.*
> *People talking without speaking,*
> *People hearing without listening,*
> *People writing songs that voices never share*
> *And no one dare*
> *Disturb the sound of silence.*

But communication need not be like this at all. The first area to focus on is the all-important skill of listening attentively. For when you listen attentively to a member of your family, not only is it likely that you will understand them better, but they are also likely to feel much better about you. In addition, your obvious interest will be making them feel better about themselves.

Listening within a family is sometimes part of a negotiating process in which both parties want to feel that their needs and point of view have been genuinely recognized by the other side. We all want to feel understood. Even when you are taking issue with the other person or presenting a contradictory point of view, you are likely to make much more headway if you can identify areas of agreement between you, or even just acknowledge the other person's perspective.

Small signals, such as nods, smiles, the occasional 'uh huh' or 'I see', if used appropriately, can all put the speaker at ease and make him feel heard. A study of what people want from listeners suggested that while their first priority was for listeners to put their own thoughts aside and be open-minded, they also want listeners to respond appropriately to what is being said rather than listening in silence.

Research suggests that there are three components to attentive listening: attending, following and reflecting. 'Attending' mainly involves your body posture; 'following' requires occasional indications that you are still alert and understanding what is being said; 'reflecting' means showing some kind of emotional engagement in what is being said.

Next time you are listening to one of your family members tell you something, try some of the following approaches.

Attending: ▷ Stop what you are doing.
  ▷ Face the person.
  ▷ Maintain eye contact.

> Lean slightly towards the person (without getting too close or crowding him).
> If listening to a child, get down to her level.

Following:
> Focus on what the person is saying, not how he is saying it.
> From time to time make sure you show your interest by saying things such as, 'Mmm', 'Really?' or 'Please go on'.
> Be patient and check your understanding of what is being said from time to time.
> Avoid asking too many questions.
> Avoid jumping to conclusions.
> Pick up non-verbal cues that suggest a response from you would be helpful: for example, a slight hesitation or a brief moment of eye contact.
> Try not to let your mind wander.

Reflecting:
> Try to empathize, imagining what it is like to be in the other person's shoes. Draw her out.
> Reflect feelings back by saying things such as, 'It sounds like you had a really tough day at school'.
> Rephrase things to be sure you have understood: 'So would I be right in thinking that you would like to postpone our holiday this year?'

In the words of the Simon and Garfunkel song, remember to listen to the sound of silence. The amazing thing is that the more you put your attentive listening skills into practice, the more people will want to talk to you, and the fewer misunderstandings you will have within your family.

As part of good listening, it is often necessary to check that you have understood. Maybe your partner says that they would really like to go to the beach at the weekend. If they are the kind of kind of person who has twenty good ideas before breakfast (see pages 12–13 for more on personality type), you might want to check that going to the beach is not just one of a number of thoughts they have had about how you might spend the day. Asking 'Can I just check that you really want to go to the beach rather than do anything else?' should clarify the situation.

Checking understanding is especially important when listening to children because they are not always able to express what they are really feeling or thinking. By checking – 'You seem to be saying that you are finding your piano lessons really difficult' – you can avoid misunderstanding vital facts that they are trying to communicate.

Make sure you have been heard

Of course it is not enough simply to have understood others; you also need to know that you have been understood by them. Communication is very much a two-way process. In my home there is an informal rule of three that we apply to checking that the children have heard general announcements we make. It goes like this. The first time you say something, such as 'Supper's ready' or 'Time to turn off the TV', you assume it has not been heard, so you say it again. This time you assume that it has been heard, but is being quietly ignored. The third time you say it, there seems to be an active response, so it has presumably been heard in the true sense of that word.

You could say that this means I am an ineffective parent who should get better at following through with my children when I say something the first time. However, I am also a parent of the real world. This means that for some general announcements I am happy to allow a certain amount of laxity so that things don't get too regimented. I would not do the same if I were having a one-to-one conversation with a member of my family.

Do you recognize the following mini-exchange?

> **Parent**: Are we agreed, then?
> **Child**: What do you mean?
> **Parent**: Are you happy with what we've been discussing?
> **Child**: Yeah, whatever.
> **Parent**: So what are you going to do next, then?
> **Child**: What are you on about?
> **Parent**: You haven't been listening to a word I've said, have you?

If you want to make sure that you have been understood, it will help if you check from the beginning rather than leaving it to the end of a conversation. This is quite straightforward and can be done without having to interrupt your child. You just need to have a number of simple questions up your sleeve, such as: 'Can I just check that…?' 'Are you saying that…?' 'Are you sure that…?' 'When you say…do you mean…?'

How to ask good questions

'Checking-type' questions are just one variety that you might want to use with your family. If you think your questioning technique needs no improvement, stop and think for a moment about the response you get to asking 'How was your day?' Nine times out of ten it produces next to nothing. However, if instead you say: 'Tell me about your day' or 'You look like you've had a good/bad day' or 'How did your maths exam go?', you are much more likely to achieve a better result. In short, if you avoid the possibility of a one-word answer ('good' or 'bad') and take a more specific interest, showing a bit more understanding, you are likely to get a fuller response. Of course, this does mean that you have to remember what your child, partner or spouse has been doing during the day...

The poet Rudyard Kipling (1865–1936) wrote of having a number of questioning words as his servants:

> *I keep six honest serving-men,*
> *(They taught me all I knew);*
> *Their names are What and Why and When*
> *And How and Where and Who.*

These six words are certainly helpful ones to use. But different situations will call for different types of question. If you need a simple factual answer without extra explanation, asking questions beginning with 'Did..., Have..., Will..., Can...?' should help, as should using any of Kipling's 'honest serving-men'.

Yes/no questions are sometimes known as closed questions because they can be answered only shortly, often by yes or no. Open questions, on the other hand, invite longer and more detailed answers. They often start with 'Why...?' and 'How...?'

Types of question

The world is full of questions, but there are just three main types.

Questions of fact. These tend to have only one correct answer. Examples include: 'What is the name of your sister?' 'What did you do yesterday?' The more complex the area, however, the more complex the answer will be: 'Why do objects fall to the ground?' While you may know that it is to do with gravity, you may not be able (or willing) to give the full details.

Questions of interpretation. These normally have more than one answer. For instance: 'Why do children tend to take after their parents?' There may be right or wrong answers, but these kinds of question encourage points of view.

Questions of judgement. These deliberately ask for some kind of opinion, belief or point of view. They have no wrong answers. 'Who's your favourite TV soap character?' 'What are the best ways of getting better at homework?' This last category of question gives most scope for an individual to explore his or her views.

There are also ' leading questions', a subdivision of the three main types above, in which the answer is being deliberately suggested:

'Would you allow your child to be taught at a school that does not believe in discipline?' The question is posed in such a way as to guide you towards the desired response.

To help you decide how to get better at asking questions, here are some more questions.

- Are you looking for a yes/no answer?
- Do you know the answer yourself?
- Why are you asking the question? Is it because you genuinely want to know the answer (which you do not currently know)? Or is it designed to test someone else's understanding?
- What kind of question is it?
- What would be the best word to start your question?
- What follow-up questions could you have ready to ask?

Often it helps to practise your questions beforehand.

Principle 4: Use more than words

We are all born with a great need to be touched. In fact, newborn babies need touch as much as they need food. Studies in orphanages and hospitals have made us aware that infants lose weight if deprived of skin contact. They may become ill and even die.

It's easy to forget that your skin just happens to be the largest organ in your body. It covers about 1.7 sq m (19 sq ft) and weighs about 3.6 kg (8 lb) in a grown man. A piece of skin the size of a 2-pence coin has more than 3 million cells, 300 or so sweat glands, some fifty nerve endings and 90 cm (3 ft) of blood vessels. For most of us, the touch of another person's skin feels good. Some people repress their craving for warmth and affection, while others go to extremes to obtain it.

Many of our adult responses depend on how we were nurtured during our infancy. We have all experienced times when the touch of a hand on our shoulder or a reassuring hug reduced our anxiety or loneliness. Touching is a powerful way of showing love and communicating without words.

Children give and receive touch frequently, but as we grow older we tend to give and receive less and less. This may be because media reports of child abuse make us fear that our gestures will be misinterpreted as sexual, or be symptomatic of our increasingly detached modern society.

Physical touch, used sensitively and appropriately, can be a powerful kind of communication and a key way of bonding as a family. British culture tends to be rather formal, so we are often uncomfortable about physical contact. One study in the 1960s showed the contrast between cultures by counting the number of touches exchanged by pairs of people sitting in coffee shops around the world:

Place	Touches per hour
San Juan, Puerto Rico	180
Paris, France	110
Gainesville, Florida	2
London, England	0

While we Brits may be less buttoned up nowadays, I suspect that we are still a long way down in the touching stakes. Perhaps our physical detachment partly reflects our psychological need for autonomy and independence.

Studies have also demonstrated how important touch can be in promoting good relationships between parents and their children, especially boys, who tend to be better adjusted in adolescence if they come from tactile and physically demonstrative families. At this time parents and teenagers tend to withdraw from one another out of a sense of self-consciousness. Hugging and kissing may stop completely at the very time when a teenager is yearning for affection. We should not be surprised, then, if teenagers use indiscriminate sex as a way of exploring their touch needs.

Of course individuals vary in their desire and need for physical contact, and other family members need to be sensitive to this.

The fact that touch is often the gateway to your emotions perhaps helps to explain its power. Touching your child or your partner is one immediate way in which you can convey your positive feelings for them.

Indeed, emotions are a kind of language in themselves. To be happy, human beings need to have positive emotional experiences, for happiness is itself a combination of positive emotions. And these are essential to effective family relationships.

Banking your emotions

American author Stephen Covey uses a helpful metaphor – the emotional bank account – to explain this point. As with a monetary bank account, deposits and withdrawals can be made, but each person's emotional bank account must be kept adequately topped up so that they feel sufficiently loved and valued. So, for example, if you constantly make demands on your partner but never give support back to him or her, the relationship may not work well.

Covey puts it like this: 'One of the biggest problems in many family cultures is the reactive tendency to continually make withdrawals instead of deposits.'

He suggests that there are four practical ways in which you can 'make deposits': being kind, apologizing, being loyal to people who are not with you, and making and keeping promises. Here are some examples of what this might mean.

Showing kindness: Lending something of yours to help another member of the family; getting up early to make breakfast for someone who has to get to work early; going to the shops to buy something that you know your child needs and surprising him with it; making time to listen to someone's problems when you are very busy.

Saying sorry (especially important for parents): Apologizing if you lose your temper; admitting when you make a mistake; making sure that all the family knows you were wrong and your child was right.

Being loyal: Showing by what you do that you will never talk about another member of the family behind their back; sticking up for absent members of the family if anyone is critical of them; always trying to describe people in the most positive way.

Making and keeping promises (especially important for parents): Thinking carefully about the needs of those around you, planning to do special things with each member of the family, then actually doing them.

'Paying in' to your family's emotional bank account is at the heart of effective and trusting communication. Once you have become aware of its importance, it is something that you can easily practise until it becomes a habit.

How can you boost your family's emotional bank account?

▶ Stop and think about your own family for a moment. Using the four ideas above, see how many ideas you can come up with for making deposits in the family's emotional bank account, then try some of them out.

Principle 5: Make time

How often do you hear yourself saying or thinking: 'I haven't got time to...'? Are you frequently too busy to do the things you really want to? How do you feel when someone you love goes out of their way to spend time with you doing things that you really enjoy?

You can see where this line of questioning is going. Spending time with someone you love, doing things that you both choose to do and giving that person your undivided attention is one of the most important aspects of any relationship. In fact, someone coined the phrase 'quality time' to describe this situation. I must confess that I don't like the term, but I definitely value the concept behind it.

Of course, everyone is busy in contemporary families, and there is an added complexity with step-families. Sometimes it seems that there just aren't enough hours in the day for children to spend time with each of their birth parents and, where appropriate, with one or more step-parent and other members of their extended family. In fact, with a bit of creativity, parents can find that they are able to give their undivided attention to their child more effectively because it has to be planned in advance. This is one potential benefit of 'split' families.

Spending time together is a key part of effective communication because to say what is really important takes time. You sometimes need to build up to it so that the moment feels right.

In all families it is helpful to create situations in which everyone can be heard on a regular basis. This is especially important for younger or quieter members of the family, who can all too easily get squeezed out, but who need 'air-time' just like everyone else. When there are important issues to be discussed within the family, they need to be given a proper airing.

You might like to set aside time with family members to discuss the things that are important to you. Make sure there are no distractions: let the answering machine take any phone calls, and set aside the ironing or next week's shopping list. It's difficult to have important conversations while you are trying to do something else. It's much better to find a setting in which you can concentrate on what the other person is saying and where you can see each other. Remember, scientists estimate that only 7 per cent of our communication consists of what we actually say.

How to ensure a fair hearing

Here are two ideas to make sure that everyone gets some uninterrupted talking time.

The talking spoon: If you have read William Golding's novel *Lord of the Flies* (1954), you may remember how a group of children is shipwrecked on an island without any adults, and the experience teaches them many things about human nature. Early on they realize that if they all talk at the same time in meetings, no one will be able to hear anything, so they come up with a rule that only the person holding a specified conch shell is allowed speak and everyone else has to listen.

The 'talking spoon' is the equivalent of the conch. If there is a clamour of noise when the family is together, having an object (a wooden spoon) that must be held by the speaker while everyone else listens ensures that each family member gets a chance to air their views while others listen in silence.

The family meeting: This is just what its name suggests. In most families there is a certain amount of stuff that needs to be talked through. There are recurring things, such as sharing out the chores and getting ready for school, and exceptional things, such as deciding where you want to go on holiday or sharing out extra tasks if someone is ill. At family meetings each person is expected and encouraged to speak up.

As with more formal meetings, some kind of agenda is helpful. A simple way of organizing this is to keep a piece of paper stuck to the fridge and encourage all members of the family to add anything they want to talk about. Setting an agenda for your conversation helps to ensure that you don't get pulled off course or try to address too many topics at one sitting.

Once a week or once a fortnight seems to be about the right frequency for family meetings, although it is always possible to call a special one if someone feels there is something important to discuss. It is also helpful to make a simple list of what is agreed at a meeting and put it up somewhere that everyone can see.

Some might think that meetings are just a bit too organized, especially if the family is very small or includes very young children. But many families find the regular and predictable format of a meeting is just what is needed to sort out all the things that need to be agreed whenever a group of people lives together.

As with the talking spoon, a key element of the family meeting is the way it allows each member to be treated with respect and gives them a chance to be listened to without interruption. In families where children (or adults for that matter) find it difficult to take turns or make their views heard, the 'talking spoon' idea can be incorporated into meetings.

Well-run family meetings give children an opportunity to develop invaluable communication, problem-solving and negotiating skills. Many routine difficulties and conflicts can be pre-empted if concerns are addressed before they escalate, and family members feel that their concerns are being taken seriously.

Different kinds of talk

The five principles we have explored in this chapter hold good for communication between members of a family pretty much regardless of age (babies excepted). But clearly, children and young people of different ages have slightly different needs, and there are some specific issues that apply to communication between adults and children.

The Swiss psychologist Jean Piaget (1897–1980) was the first to draw attention to the fact that only as children get older and become more sophisticated can they deal competently with more abstract concepts. You may have observed parents of pre-school children going into elaborate explanations about why certain behaviour is wrong and wondered whether anything is getting through to the child. It probably isn't, as the child is not developmentally equipped to process what is being said.

Effective communication needs to be relevant and appropriate in content and style to the person being addressed. With very small children aged between, say, two and seven, it is best if you keep things practical and simple: 'Do this, please', 'Please don't do...', 'If you touch this, it will...' These are simple sentences of the 'the cat sat on the mat' variety, and the responses will be equally simple: 'Why's the cat sitting on the mat, Mummy?' All the while, try to remember that the small child is at the centre of her world, and the more you can do this and give simple explanations that allow the child to see things from her point of view, the better. During their early years, children are learning to group practical things together, even to categorize them. For example, spherical objects are 'balls' and things that move tend to be 'cars'. But they are less likely to be able to think about concepts, such as time, kindness and fair play.

Once children are at primary school, they begin to become better at seeing different points of view, at using numbers and at grasping key concepts. And once they graduate to secondary school, they can cope with much more advanced concepts, ideas and arguments.

As children get older, they appreciate that there must be give and take for families to run effectively, and that it becomes increasingly helpful to bargain. Look at the exchange below.

Child: Can I have a lift into town?
Dad: Sure. If you help me with this clearing up, I'll run you in when we have finished.

Communication is one of the social skills we all must learn, and research has shown that being socially skilled is likely to lead to greater happiness.

Troubleshooting

Here are some frequent family-related problems. As always, the answers are signposts for possible action, not hard and fast rules.

I find it impossible to talk to my ex-partner.

Many people feel like this. First, you might like to identify those areas that require you to maintain communication. The chances are they are probably to do with children and/or money. If things between you are difficult, stick to these areas and try to maintain a practical, problem-solving approach to the issues concerned. E-mail can be a less emotive way of conveying necessary information to each other. If face-to-face contact is necessary, the presence of a mutually trusted third party can help everyone to keep their cool.

If your relationship is over, it is not necessary for you to be the best of friends, but ongoing bitterness and resentment between you are likely to be destructive to both parties. They can also adversely affect any children you have, so try to maintain a civil relationship. If unresolved tensions from the past are clogging up channels of communication in the present, it may be worth seeking mediation from Relate (see page 214) or a professional counsellor – not to repair the marriage, but to help clear the air in a safe context so that both of you can move on and reduce the level of acrimony in your dealings with each other.

Family mealtimes always turn into family arguments.

This tends to suggest that there are communication and behaviour issues that need to be addressed in some other context, such as a regular family meeting (see page 44). If family members know that things will be dealt with rather than ignored, they are much more likely to be prepared to put their frustrations to one side and have a pleasant enough mealtime together.

You may also need some ground rules for mealtimes to make sure that they are regular, routine events and not the only context in which everyone spends time together. Otherwise, it is inevitable that underlying tensions will erupt at these points.

I hate being hugged or touched.

Well, it isn't compulsory, but you are missing out. Other family members need to be aware that this is an issue for you and that they need to respect your personal space and perhaps find alternative ways to express their affection.

One way to become more relaxed about touch is to build up your exposure gradually and systematically through desensitization exercises with your partner or a good massage therapist. The idea is that you increase your tolerance to touch in stages on the understanding that you control the rate and duration of exposure. If something has happened to you in the past that makes you particularly protective of your physical boundaries, it is a good idea to seek help and not let those experiences deprive you of what is an important human need.

I can't seem to make time to talk to my partner.

If this is really the case, I am tempted to say that your priorities are a bit askew. It might be a cliché that few of us on our deathbed will regret not spending more time at our job, but many will suddenly realize how much they will miss those nearest to them. Make a real effort to decide what is most important to you in life and try to allocate your resources accordingly.

If there are unspoken tensions between you and your partner, it can feel easier not to talk, and people become very good at using the 'business' of daily life as a means of avoiding difficult conversations.

Moving on

In this chapter we have seen how some simple principles can help you become better at communicating with the other members of your family. And we have learnt that communication consists of more than talking. As the author Ernest Hemingway (1899–1961) once remarked: 'I like to listen. I have learned a great deal from listening carefully. Most people never listen.'

Now let's plunge right into the heart of it all, to explore some of the things that make relationships work better.

CHAPTER 3 Understanding Relationships

When I was a boy of fourteen, my father was so ignorant I could hardly stand to have the old man around. But when I got to be twenty-one, I was astonished by how much he'd learned in seven years.

Mark Twain, author (1835–1910)

What do you know about how relationships work? Here are some questions to get you thinking. As before, you might like to think them through with your partner or a close friend.

- What do you most admire in people?
- What irritates you most in people?
- How many important relationships do you have?
- Which are the most important relationships in your life?
- Which are the most important relationships in your family?
- Which are the relationships that you need to work at most at the moment?
- Which are the most difficult relationships, and why?
- How confident are you in your own understanding of relationships?

It is has often been said that you can choose your friends but not your family, and this is essentially true. Consequently, understanding the ways you can improve your family relationships is extremely important.

In today's complex family set-ups there are many different potential relationships. Alongside the usual parent, grandparent, sibling, uncle, aunt and cousin relationships, there are those brought about by families that are 'blended' together after a divorce or separation. Many children have to deal not just with their own natural siblings, but with stepbrothers and stepsisters. They also have to come to terms with step-parents. And parents must continue to have a relationship with ex-partners because the interests of their children require them to communicate. Many families also have friends who are almost part of the family, undertaking childcare and other responsibilities.

Add to these complicated set-ups the fact that growing children need to challenge those around them as a natural part of their development and you can see why many people find keeping the peace and managing their relationships at home a challenging and exhausting part of life.

Inevitably, we spend a lot of time with our family. In fact, as a result of the UK 2000 Time Use Survey, we know a bit more about what we all get up to. This survey, the first of its kind, gives us an interesting picture of life in the first decade of the twenty-first century.

HOW WE SPEND OUR TIME... AND OUR LEISURE

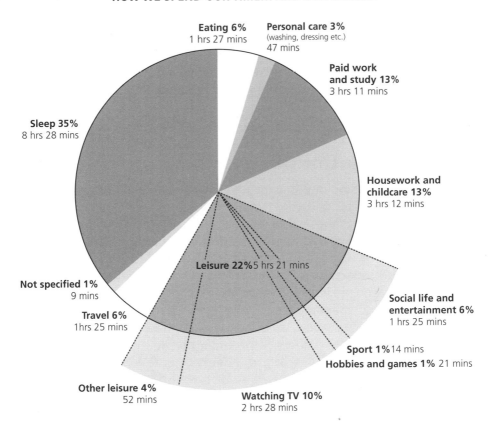

Eating 6%
1 hrs 27 mins

Personal care 3%
(washing, dressing etc.)
47 mins

Paid work
and study 13%
3 hrs 11 mins

Sleep 35%
8 hrs 28 mins

Housework and
childcare 13%
3 hrs 12 mins

Leisure 22% 5 hrs 21 mins

Not specified 1%
9 mins

Social life and
entertainment 6%
1 hrs 25 mins

Travel 6%
1hrs 25 mins

Sport 1% 14 mins
Hobbies and games 1% 21 mins

Other leisure 4%
52 mins

Watching TV 10%
2 hrs 28 mins

These figures are averages for all adults, and include weekends as well as weekdays, hence the comparatively low amount of time spent on work.

The survey shows that couples spend about two and a half hours together a day – an average based on two hours during the week and three and a half hours at weekends. The most common shared activity is – you guessed it – watching TV.

The time spent by men and women on most activities is similar, except that women still do nearly double the amount of housework.

This is the current context for families in the UK, and it is broadly similar in most other developed countries.

If I were to attempt a mischievous summary, it might go like this. We live in increasingly complex family units, spending a third of our life sleeping (except when we have young children), a third working (in either paid employment or household chores), and the remaining third slumped in front of the television. In that scenario, what possible chance is there for relationships to thrive in the modern family?

Of course, there is much more to it than this. To begin with there are certain things we know about the way relationships work (and don't work) that it may be helpful to understand. Let's start by exploring personality in a little more depth, finding out a bit more about the emotional component of relationships, and looking at some of the ways to avoid common family problems.

Effective relationships

In Chapter 1 you found out how the Myers-Briggs Type Indicator® assesses different personalities, discovered some of the key characteristics associated with each of them, and a few of the ways in which they can affect relationships. Now we need to explore another dimension of personality.

Within each of us there is a kind of Jekyll and Hyde split. On the one hand there are aspects of ourselves that we come to value and promote as features of our preferred identity. Psychologists Hal and Zidra Stone refer to this set of characteristics as the 'primary self'. So, depending on influences in my background, I might end up emphasizing certain features of my personality over others – for example, deliberately identifying myself with traits such as resilience, energy and ambition that fit with my family's notion of what it means to be successful in life. Alternatively, I might rebel against my family's value system and embrace a more laid-back persona that deliberately prioritizes connectedness with other people over professional achievement.

However, in order to promote certain characteristics, we have to bury or 'disown' other aspects of ourselves that we feel are incompatible with them. If I view myself as a tough, no-nonsense negotiator, what do I do with the part of me that can feel weak or vulnerable, or can empathize with another's distress? The answer, according to the psychologists, is that these parts of myself get pushed below the surface of awareness where collectively they represent aspects of my 'disowned self'.

What's your preferred personality?

Take a moment to think about yourself and how you would like others to see you.

▷ Make a list of all the words that spring to mind, then write their opposite in a second column. Have a look at the list of paired words below to give you a start.

Careful	Risk-taker
Emotional	Rational
Wild	Restrained
Tidy	Messy
Outgoing	Shy
Intellectual	Unintellectual
Creative	Predictable
Spontaneous	Controlled
Loud	Quiet
Sporty	Unsporty
Glamorous	Ordinary
Calm	Frenetic
Social	Private

In your own list, the words in your first column probably relate to aspects of your primary self, whereas those in the second are likely to represent features of your disowned self.

Our relationship with the disowned self is very mixed. At one level we are often extremely nervous around disowned-self characteristics because of the apparent threat they pose to our preferred identity. This is why we can react so strongly when we meet aspects of our disowned self in others. If you think of someone you really dislike or who always rubs you up the wrong way, the chances are that the person represents some aspect of yourself that you prefer not to acknowledge.

Alternatively, we can also distance ourselves from aspects of the disowned self by overvaluing and idealizing those characteristics in such a way that it seems impossible they could ever be anything to do with us.

However, here comes the interesting bit. Go back to your list of words and consider how many of the people who are most important to you (maybe your partner or your friends) demonstrate characteristics that you associate with your disowned self.

As you will have discovered by doing this exercise, the paradox is that we can often be strongly attracted to people who reflect features of our disowned self. This is not only because these people complement our primary self, but because through our relationship with that person we are able to validate bits of ourself that at a deeper level we know are 'missing'. This is why so often opposites do indeed attract.

The attraction of opposites is good for the long-term survival of our species because it tends to produce parents who between them have different qualities that are suited to handling different situations. However, it also presents challenges because when things go wrong for you and your primary self is challenged, the very thing that you liked in your partner may suddenly irritate you.

When we fall in love or things are going well for us, the primary self tends to relax. Under such circumstances we tend to be much more accommodating towards aspects of our disowned self in others. For the go-getting, focused individual a partner's free-spirited ditziness can be construed as endearing. However, if circumstances put pressure on our own ability to maintain our primary self (say the go-getter misses out on a crucial promotion or is unexpectedly made redundant), disowned characteristics in the other person that may previously have been experienced in a positive way can once again become irritating or threatening.

If you understand this simple but powerful view of the different and often polarized elements of your personality, and how it is affected by adverse circumstances, you may be better able to watch out for telltale signs of discomfort and understand more about why they are happening.

Emotional intelligence

Ever found yourself getting angry in a situation and not quite knowing why? Or been driven mad by someone who just doesn't seem to be recognizing how you are feeling about something? Most of us have at some time or other. The chances are that it was because the emotional element of the situation was not being handled well. I estimate that something like 80 per cent of everything that goes wrong in relationships is somehow to do with emotions. (The remaining 20 per cent involves intellect, circumstances beyond our control and so on.) Perhaps this state of affairs is not surprising in a world that places a higher value on academic success than emotional competence.

In the past decade or so we have learnt a great deal about the importance of emotional intelligence – the ability to deal with emotions effectively. Unlike our intelligence quotient (IQ), our emotional quotient (EQ) is not a fixed concept. In other words, you can get better at it.

Emotional intelligence

According to psychologist Daniel Goleman, who popularized the concept of EQ in the 1990s, emotional intelligence has five main components, each of which can help you to understand more about relationships.

1. **Knowing your emotions**

   What are you actually feeling? Can you give it a name? If you have a dull ache or a gut feeling, are you able to recognize it and describe it to yourself?

2. **Managing your emotions**

   Of course, we all have ups and downs, but can you keep your powerful emotions in check? Or do you give way to angry shouting, undignified tantrums or huge sulks? When someone is driving slowly and you are in a hurry, do you suffer from road rage? Do you get so anxious about your children that you almost cease to function? When you are in a bad mood, do you know how to get yourself out if it?

3. **Motivating yourself**

   Do you manage to stay positive, harnessing your emotions so that you keep going, even when things are difficult? Are you resilient?

4. **Recognizing other people's emotions**

   Can you empathize with other people? Do you notice other people's emotions building? Can you think of things to say that show you have noticed what someone is thinking without further inflaming the situation?

5. **Handling relationships**

   When faced with your own and other people's emotions, can you handle them without losing your self-control? Are you able to be true to your own emotions without swamping other people's? Are you comfortable when other people show strong emotions? Are you able to negotiate and listen?

The more you are able to answer 'yes' to these questions, the more developed your EQ is likely to be (or the more deluded you are).

Emotional intelligence is undoubtedly an important part of what it is to understand relationships, and, most importantly, of putting this understanding into practice in your family life.

Seeing the bigger picture

Family relationships take place within increasingly complex circumstances, and all those relationships affect each other. From the work of therapists we know that families can have agendas and needs that exert a subtle but real influence over the behaviour of the individuals within them.

Sometimes problems within the family group, such as a child's aggressive tantrums, may provide a focus of concern for both parents that temporarily unites them and provides a welcome distraction from underlying tensions in the relationship between them.

Individuals may also play certain roles – the joker, the fix-it person or the scapegoat, for example – that seem to meet a need within the family system, but can prove restrictive for the person concerned. You need to be aware of this kind of pattern and help family members to break out of their traditional 'scripts' if relationships within the family are to remain fresh and fulfilling. (Find out more about the roles we all play on pages 101–14.)

You also need to stay alert to patterns in relationships that may unhelpfully exclude others. A family belief that 'Mark is such a daddy's boy' may be true, but it could also seem to imply that the son has the first call on his father's attention. This, in turn, might prevent his sister from forming a closer relationship with her father, or restrict her participation in certain activities. It could even limit the full development of the mother/son relationship.

Conversely, an overdeveloped alliance between, for example, a mother and her daughter may disempower the father, impair his status and compromise his position to parent effectively. Sometimes alliances need to be strengthened (between partners or siblings) in order to keep relations within the family running smoothly.

From time to time problems from the outside world can be imported into your relationships within the family. A child's moody and belligerent behaviour in the home may reflect things that are going on for him in his peer group at school. His behaviour can be seen as a way of expressing his concerns about relationships outside the family, and is likely to have a significant (and negative) impact on what is happening at home.

The important thing is to try to think creatively and be aware that no relationship exists in isolation from others. Sometimes the place where the problems pop up does not reflect the true source of them, and only a broader perspective equips you to deal with them effectively.

Of course, all this is going on while a whole host of other things over which you have no control, such as teenage hormones, the weather, noisy neighbours, may all be very much in evidence.

Five principles of making relationships work

There are five general principles you need to bear in mind to make relationships work effectively.

Principle 1: Know yourself and those close to you

You have already seen how there is a connection between happiness and an understanding of yourself. The same is true for relationships, although in this case it goes further still, requiring you to have a better knowledge of close family members.

The more you understand yourself – how you react to situations, what you believe in – the better you are likely to be at relating to others, and the easier they will find it to relate to you. Of course, who you are is a very big question and one that philosophers, writers and psychologists have been wrestling with over the ages. You have just found out a bit about your primary and disowned selves, and may be feeling that getting to grips with EQ is just too complicated. Don't be put off.

What can EQ do for you?

At its simplest level, understanding EQ will help you to say what is really important to you and what drives you mad. Try this exercise to see if it helps you to clarify your thinking.

Turn-ons: What do you care about and like? Use these words to prompt you:

causes	issues	situations	activities
food	places	sayings	behaviour

Hot buttons: What really irritates you and makes you angry? Use the same words above to generate some ideas.

▷ Write these words down. What do they tell you about yourself? Do they help?

▷ Now draw a simple chart of the people in your family who matter most to you. Just focus on those with whom you spend a lot of time. Write up to five key words about your turn-ons and hot buttons for each person (see the example overleaf).

Michael   Kind
                 Calm
                 Distracted
                 Lazy

Isabel   Happy
                 Energetic
                 Scatterbrained
                 Gossipy

This whole exercise can be done as a family game, a bit like the TV show where couples are asked questions about each other's likes and dislikes to see how well they know each other. The advantage of being open about all this and treating it as a game is that it keeps things light and prevents individual family members becoming defensive, especially about their hot buttons.

The point of it all is to suggest that the more you know your own and other people's likes and dislikes, the better you can become at trying to create situations at home where you avoid people's hot buttons and do things from which as many people as possible derive pleasure.

You cannot completely avoid everyone's hot buttons, especially where these involve behaviours that are not especially helpful. For example, if a father's hot button is 'situations where his children disagree with him', it is probably important for him to wise up to modern parenting a bit rather than feel justified in responding angrily to those situations. There may, however, be moments when it is not appropriate to disagree with your father, such as in front of the grandparents or at school, and this can be talked about and agreed as part of the activity.

Another useful result of an activity like this is the opportunity it produces for everyone to let others know what they feel strongly about. Self-expression is an important aspect of happy family life, even if it produces tricky moments. It is much better to tackle issues quickly rather than letting them fester. If not addressed, they can easily build into resentment on a scale that may be difficult to manage when it eventually erupts. Unexpressed resentment can also contaminate relationships in more subtle ways. It seeps out in the form of nagging or teasing, or may be turned inwards, in which case it may foster depression and anxiety.

How well do you know your partner?

Being open about emotions and trying to understand more about yourself and those close to you is an important and inevitably challenging part of living together in a family. Some interesting research in this area has come up with an idea called 'attachment theory'. This describes the infant's tendency to seek closeness to another person (normally its mother) and feel secure when that person is present.

In a secure attachment relationship, children want to be physically close to their carer and tend to become unhappy if separated from that person for long periods. Securely attached children want to be with their carer if they sense danger or feel anxious. However, the knowledge that their attachment figure will protect them also makes it safe for infants to explore the world and tolerate limited periods of separation.

If you watch a very young child, you will see how he wants to be constantly attached to his mother. If the mother goes out of the room, the child reacts – usually by crying. As the child grows up, he generally learns not to become over-anxious about departure because Mummy invariably returns.

However, this is not always the case. Many factors can influence the nature of our early relationship with key attachment figures. What psychologists have learnt is that the patterns and role models we experience in our early relationships, especially during the first two years, can have a significant effect on the way we continue to relate to people in our adult life.

Depending on what happens to you during your early childhood, you tend to form one of three styles of attachment – secure, avoidant or anxious.

Secure adults find it relatively easy to get close to others. They are comfortable when they depend on others and when others depend on them. Secure adults don't often worry about being abandoned or about someone getting close to them.

Avoidant adults are often uncomfortable when they are close to others. They find it difficult to trust others completely or to allow themselves to depend on others. They tend to be nervous and uncomfortable when anyone gets too close or intimate with them.

Anxious adults find that others are reluctant to get as close to them as they would like. They often worry that their partner doesn't really love them or won't want to stay with them. Anxious adults want to merge completely with another person. Not surprisingly, this sometimes scares people away.

What attachment type are you?

- Do you recognize any attachment type in terms of your own behaviour or in the behaviour of those around you?
- Can you identify any recurrent patterns in your relationships with others? What was your relationship with your own parents like and how might it have influenced you in your attitudes and behaviour towards others?
- How do you react in a crisis? Do you seek help from others? Do you withdraw into yourself and work it out alone/go to pieces?
- How easy do you find it to trust other people?

How can you use attachment theory?

There are several reasons why understanding attachment theory might help you to create a happier family.

- Adults who are anxious or avoidant with regard to attachment find it much harder to cope with the challenges of life in general and interpersonal relationships in particular.
- There is a high degree of correlation between the attachment status or type of parent and the likely status of their children. In four out of five cases, one predicts the other. In other words, if you are an anxiously attached parent, it is likely that your child will demonstrate an anxious attachment style too.
- For most of us, the way in which we learn to manage anxiety early in life will continue unless our circumstances change or we do something to change our established pattern. If we always coped with difficult situations by rushing to our mother for protection, it is likely that we may continue to look for similar safety in others throughout our life.
- Knowing what we have a tendency to do and why is half the battle. It is the automatic nature of our attachment behaviours that can create problems, but if we have some level of insight, we can make different choices and moderate our behaviour.
- Some specific problems resulting from insecure attachment can be managed by learning ways of compensating or deliberately exposing ourselves to experiences that allow us to develop more secure attachment styles. For example, if you feel low self-esteem, you might choose to go to an assertiveness class, or catalogue your achievements, or canvass the opinions of friends and loved ones.

If you are unable to deal with stress and anxiety, you might like to try self-help, such as taking up yoga or learning to meditate. Or you could alert your partner to the warning signs so that he or she can help you before you reach meltdown.

If you have difficulty with trusting people, you might want to be more explicit with your partner about this, and ask for help and understanding. Knowing that you do not doubt your partner's trustworthiness may help them to help you.

If you feel unable to support your partner, you might find it helpful to set specific time aside simply to listen to him or her. You can then think about the challenges to be faced by your partner during the week and plan ahead how you can best offer support. Find out what helps your partner and what doesn't.

And if resolving conflict is difficult, you could decide to go on a course to help you get better at managing conflict and negotiating.

Principle 2: Express feelings openly

In A.A. Milne's *Winnie the Pooh* (1926) there is the following exchange:

> Piglet sidled up to Pooh from behind. 'Pooh!' he whispered.
> 'Yes, Piglet?'
> 'Nothing,' said Piglet, taking Pooh's paw. 'I just wanted to be sure of you.'

We are all like Piglet, really. There is an element of insecure attachment in every one of us. We want to be sure of those around us, sure that we are loved. But sometimes this is difficult. Love is replaced by distress or fear or even anger. Something goes wrong with our emotions, and our relationships founder. We go to sleep feeling uneasy (or lie awake worrying).

On some days it is easy to think that the world is against you. Nothing seems to go right. You argue with your family. You argue with colleagues at work. You get angry. Others get angry. Someone walks out after throwing a big tantrum. And that's just the adults!

Or maybe it's different for you. No tantrums or tears, but a stiff upper lip and a seething discontent inside. As you go through your day, your stomach feels tight and you feel stressed. Ordinary things make you react in unhelpful ways.

In either of these two scenarios it's easy to forget that life need not be like this. You might feel that you are being 'forced' into behaving in certain ways, but this is not so. No one can tell you how you feel and no one can force you to behave in particular ways (except in extremely unusual circumstances). We can all make choices that change the way we act. The simple truth is that expressing emotions openly promotes a sense of well-being and reduces tension. It helps us to recover from hurtful experiences, and also helps others to understand us.

Of course, there are times when displays of emotion aren't helpful, but hiding or holding back your feelings can ultimately affect your physical and mental health. It certainly damages relationships. Even arguments are healthy as long as they don't become unpleasant. In fact, learning to disagree without making someone else unhappy is an important part of any relationship.

So next time you catch yourself saying something such as, 'He made me do it', stop and think again. You are the person who decides what you do and it all starts with your emotions.

Three steps to better emotional health

It is possible to manage your emotions more effectively in the family (and elsewhere). Just follow these simple steps.

Step 1: Recognize the emotions you are feeling

We all learn to talk with the help of our parents and family. By the time we go to school we have a vocabulary running into several thousand words. And by the time we leave secondary education, our vocabulary has grown to several tens of thousands. Yet although we are confident users of a great many words, we seem strangely reluctant and unconfident when it comes to using the comparatively small number of words widely available to describe our emotions. Try this.

▶ Here is a list of words beginning with the letters A–F. Take a moment to consider how many of these words you use on a regular basis within your family.

> Afraid Aggressive Ambivalent Apologetic Angry Anxious
> Bewildered Bored
> Confused Curious
> Defensive Disgusted Distressed
> Embarrassed Entertained Excited
> Fearful Frail Furious

▶ How many more can you think of for the rest of the alphabet? Does your list run to fifty? A hundred?

▷ Now think back over the previous week. Which of the words you have come up with describe emotions that you have felt? What was the situation in which you felt them? American psychologist Dr Silvan Tomkins believed that all feelings could be grouped into the following nine types.

Interest
Surprise
Anger
Joy
Fear
Distress
Disgust
Dissmell
Shame

You may not recognize the word 'dissmell'. Tomkins invented it to describe the natural response to unpleasant smells (a wrinkling of the nose and grimacing of the face – a bit like disgust). Sometimes emotions combine to make an even more powerful one. A good example of this is contempt, a combination of anger and dissmell. This is a particularly nasty and destructive emotion.

You may already have noticed something significant about this list of words: there are more negative emotions than positive ones. Perhaps this is a cultural thing, or maybe we are just less good at labelling and differentiating positive emotions. This whole area is a major challenge for us all because if we are not able to deal with feelings that are eating us up, we will feel unhappy. Interestingly, if we are unable to express positive emotions, we may also be unhappy because none of our nearest and dearest will know what we are feeling and will therefore be unable to share our joy or pleasure.

Step 2: Talk about your emotions.

Assuming that you know what you are feeling, it really helps to talk about it. But many people find this difficult. As you read this book, you may be thinking that it's all very well to agree this in principle, but much more difficult in practice. Perhaps you grew up in a family where expressing emotion was frowned upon. Or possibly you have had a negative experience recently when you laid open your feelings to someone and felt that they betrayed your confidence by telling someone else. Or maybe you are worried that those around you will not be interested in what you feel and are too busy anyway. Or perhaps you've simply not had much practice at saying how you feel.

Whatever the reason, you can learn to talk about your emotions.

▶ If you need to build up your confidence first, try writing down what you feel. Simply note on a piece of paper whatever comes into your head and heart. If you prefer to be more systematic, keep a feelings diary for a week. Each day make regular notes of what you feel and what is going on for you at that time.

▶ Or try talking to yourself if you find writing too structured. Your 'conversation' might go something like this:

Voice 1: How am I feeling today?
Voice 2: I'm feeling bewildered.
Voice 1: What's happened that I feel bewildered about?
Voice 2: Well, every time I try to help my husband with an important presentation he has to do he tells me to mind my own business. Yet he has asked me to help him because he is finding public speaking really hard and knows that I enjoy it.
Voice 1: What can I do about it?
Voice 2: I could choose a moment when he seems relaxed and check that he is really OK about it.

It may be that the husband in this example does want help but feels unable to accept it. Possibly he feels that he should be able to cope alone. Or maybe he's so stressed out that he has become incapable of thinking rationally about it. Either way, it is likely that the bewilderment being felt by the wife will be cleared up through sensitive talking and listening.

Step 3: Do something about emotions if they are bothering you

Often the mere act of talking something through is enough to sort it out. But sometimes action is required.

Assuming that you have named your feelings and begun to talk about them, here are some ways of dealing with them that seem to work.

▶ Get to the source of the problem. Something has happened and you are now feeling a response. Explore the source.

If you are afraid, establish the cause, the reasonableness of the situation, and what action you might take, as in this example.

Emotion	Reasonableness	Action
Afraid that I will lose my job.	Quite likely as the company has been making a loss for a year now.	Start actively looking for a new job and openly talking with partner about being careful with money.

In a situation like this it is quite reasonable to feel afraid. While the action may not take the fear away, it is likely to improve things.

If you are feeling unhappy, see if you can write or talk about it in detail. Or try doing something that you know normally cheers you up.

If you are angry, take some deep breaths, force yourself to count to five before responding, then deliberately speak in a calm, soft voice. Alternatively, try to dissipate your anger by doing something physical, such as going for a run. (Endorphins, the chemicals released in the brain during exercise, make you feel happier.)

When your feeling seems to arise from something done by someone else, remember this essential (and sometimes irritating) fact: no one can *make* you feel something, only *you* can.

Be clear about what has happened, how you feel and what you want, as shown in the following words from a mother to her son: 'Your music was so loud that it kept me awake last night. I am feeling disappointed because you had promised that you would turn it off at 10 p.m. Please can you make sure you turn it off promptly tonight?'

Sometimes we just feel down and it's not quite clear why. Talking can help, as can not fretting too much about it. Doing something completely different can take you out of yourself. A friend of mine reckons that everybody has the occasional low spot and that we should not worry about them. She used to allow her children up to two 'mental health' days every year. On these days, even if they were not actually ill, she would allow them not to go to school and instead spend the day with them doing something special.

The power of negative emotions

One of the reasons why I am dwelling on negative emotions in relationships is that they can so easily lead to hurt. And, unfortunately, the things we do to hurt each other have a far bigger effect on our relationships than the nice things. It is also very easy to slip into negative habits, so you need to be on the alert to spot these in your relationships.

One early warning sign is when two of you are constantly thinking the worst of each other. In such a situation, it is all too easy for emotions to escalate. An accidental lapse of memory when shopping becomes a deliberate act of nastiness. Being a few moments late home suggests an illicit affair.

It is just a small step from these symptoms to the development of contempt – an emotion that, according to international relationship expert Dr John Gottman, is almost certainly bound to lead to a relationship breaking up.

Principle 3: Give and take

You scratch my back and I'll scratch yours, goes the old saying, and with good reason. Sometimes known as 'reciprocity', give and take is seldom far from the heart of effective relationships. You help someone in the family and they help you. You give gifts and you receive them. Every successful group of human beings needs to have its giving and taking roughly in balance. If one individual or sub-group takes too much of the group's resources, resentment will build up.

In terms of relationships, we know that if they are to work, they must be seen as mutually rewarding. The majority of affairs occur in partnerships where one person doesn't feel they are being fairly treated. When one person is constantly blamed for things, it is a powerful indicator that there is something wrong in a relationship. (Look back at the idea of the emotional bank account on page 41 to remind yourself what you have already found out about this.)

Fairness, as we will see later in this book, especially in Chapter 7, does not mean that both partners have to share every task equally. What the research actually indicates is that things work best when partners develop their own areas of 'expertise' in a relationship and are allowed to get on with it. It is simply that the relative contribution has to be perceived as fair. So, for example, one person may do most of the cooking because he or she is good at it and enjoys it, while another handles the finances because he or she is better at that.

And where relationships with children are concerned, although it is an inevitable part of the responsibility of a parent to be giving more than receiving, even this cannot be allowed to become too unbalanced. A mother or father who is always preparing and clearing up meals cannot go on for ever with the younger members of the family simply arriving for food and then disappearing without ever helping.

This is not to suggest that you should become fixated on 'getting a fair deal'. In fact, research suggests that there are two types of couple. In the first type the partners give out a strong sense of mutual concern for the other. Within the second type the partners operate a much more rigid 'score sheet' approach to life, keeping a precise record of who does what. Not surprisingly, the first of these two types of relationship tends to be happier.

The important principle to be grasped is that not every task or area of responsibility has to be divided up and shared out equally for everyone to be kept happy. In fact, family relationships tend to be most harmonious when members play to their strengths. Thus a mother with a strong practical bent might prefer to take over the DIY and car maintenance, while her partner who enjoys cooking takes on the task of organizing menus and preparing the majority of family meals. The most important thing is that arrangements are seen to be fair by both parties and that there is a sense of joint participation and investment in family life.

What are your family contracts?

There is, in effect, a kind of informal contract between members of a family that defines who does what and how much give and take there is.

▷ Take a moment to explore some of the 'contracts' that exist in one or two of your own close relationships. What do you give and what do you take? Think through a typical week and use the following chart to prompt your thoughts.

MY RELATIONSHIP WITH ....

Ways I give	Ways I take

▷ What are the main ways in which you give? Are they the flip side of what you take? Or are they different in any obvious way?

If you accept the importance of the reciprocity principle in your life, it may lead you to ask some challenging questions, especially when you are in one of the many complex families (like mine) that involve step-parent relationships.

When it comes to making arrangements for children, you must obviously bear in mind what is in their best interests, but what, for example, is the appropriate amount of give and take over the way you organize transport for your children between two homes at weekends? Go too far down this route and you end up splitting Christmas Day down the middle, with no one really enjoying the experience, rather than finding an overall sense of what is 'fair'. (Alternating Christmases may be a better solution in this specific case.)

How's your give and take?

Once you start thinking about reciprocity, you might want to compare your preferences with your current reality and see what you conclude.

▷ How do you like to be treated in your relationship with your partner/daughter/ex-husband, etc?

▷ How does your experience suggest that they actually treat you?

▷ Do any of your relationships seem unbalanced? If so, how have you allowed this situation to develop?

▷ What could you do about things to shift them more into balance?

With the exception of a few extraordinary people that I can think of (the kind of people who tirelessly put themselves out for you time and time again), most of us find it easier to take than to give. So it may be worth using the exercise above to check out those relationships that seem to have a large imbalance. If you are taking too much, how about thinking of three ways in which you could give something back? Take a moment to remind yourself of just what it is that the person concerned really likes.

One of the most important ways in which you can give is by sharing positive emotions. You have just seen how important it is to talk openly about them, but in addition to this, try 'giving' interest, joy, or any positive emotion to someone you are close to and watch its effects.

Not only are you likely to find that your own positivity may be contagious, but, generally speaking, like breeds like, so demonstrating kindness and joy, for example, tends to create the same behaviour in others. (There are exceptions, of course; we have all had experiences where even unremitting optimism cannot seem to shake someone else out of their unhappiness, but it's worth trying.)

Principle 4: Spot and avoid negative cycles

It's getting late. You are due to go out for a meal with friends, but the children are still not asleep and you are upstairs trying to read a story to one of them. In fact, your partner is still not back from work, even though he said he would be home early to help with bedtime. Then the front door slams and you hear him arriving. There are sounds of the fridge being opened and the unmistakable noise of a ring-pull being removed from a can of beer. Finally, he walks upstairs and asks if you are nearly ready to go out. You are exploding with anger inside. 'Where the hell have you been?' you are thinking. 'Why is it always left to me to look after the children?'

What happens next in this example is likely to determine whether this relationship is a happy one or not.

If the man (the gender is not important and could easily be reversed) immediately apologizes, explains that things are really tough at work and he had to stay late, and then offers to let you go downstairs while he looks after the children, all is likely to be well.

Even if the man and woman have a short row, each sharing their frustrations with the other, but then jointly helping to get the children settled and sorting out the babysitter who has just arrived, the evening should not be ruined.

But if a shouting match ensues between the man and the woman, with each seeing life only from their own point of view, there are some serious issues to resolve. And if this kind of exchange happens on a regular basis, the relationship is highly likely to fail. A negative cycle of behaviour has become a habit and is slowly corroding each person's view of the other.

Negative cycles can often creep up on you unawares. A particular topic of conversation, for example, can produce predictably hostile and defensive responses from one partner who has got stuck in a rut and not yet noticed that their behaviour is becoming unhelpful.

This type of situation is pretty serious, but studies indicate that it is not necessarily the big crises that do the most harm to relationships: it's the quality of the day-to-day exchanges that can be most damaging. Criticism, negative body language, expressions of contempt and hair-trigger defensiveness all suggest future difficulties in a relationship.

Can you break the cycle of negative exchanges?

▶ Take stock of your own relationship with your partner. Are there any recurring negative cycles of behaviour that are causing you unhappiness? Think through the last week to see if anything comes to mind.

▶ Think about what can you do to avoid the negativity. You might like to try the STOP process devised by the Bristol Community Family Trust (see page 214). STOP signs are the four bad habits you need to recognize in yourself. They are not necessarily anyone's fault: they just need to be stopped because they are messing up your relationship.

The first STOP sign is S for 'scoring points'. 'You did this.' 'Well, you did that.' This is not a healthy, cooperative conversation. It's a bit like a game of table tennis, with accusations hurled back and forth to see who wins. Occasionally, it can escalate from table tennis to outright warfare. 'You left the cap off the toothpaste.' 'Well, you're not so perfect.' 'If you don't like it, then leave.'

The second STOP sign is T for 'thinking the worst'. 'He's being nice. What does he want?' Or 'She forgot the cereal I asked for. She doesn't love me.' Or 'He bought flowers. What's he done wrong?' Or 'She's doing it just to annoy me.' Something happens and you assume the worst. Yet being negative is almost never the deliberate intention. Explanations are rarely sufficient to change these negative assumptions.

The third STOP sign is O for 'opting out'. 'I give up... I just can't win with you... I'm not taking this any more... I'm off to the pub.' Opting out is where one or both people withdraw in the face of a difficult issue. This can be emotional or physical withdrawal. Men tend to opt out more often because they think women are nagging and causing conflict. In reality, women are usually just trying to talk something over. Having opted out of a discussion about money, for example, you find money a more difficult issue to discuss next time. Opting out is destructive because issues are shut down one by one until there is nothing left to discuss. Taking time out to calm down is not the same as opting out. It's helpful to take a breather to calm down so long as you return to discuss the issue.

The fourth STOP sign is P for 'putting down'. You can put somebody down in a number of ways, starting with character assassination: 'You moron...you're useless' to the more subtle 'You shouldn't think like that... Don't worry... Don't be sad'. Rolling eyes and clicking tongues have a similarly destructive effect. All these things put others down.

Learning to recognize these STOP signs in your own relationship is a good starting point. Left unchecked, STOP signs will deepen and grow, and consume your relationship.

Spotting a negative cycle of behaviour is the most important step towards stopping it and finding better ways of dealing with whatever it is that has set you off in the first place.

It will then be helpful to find a way to talk about any patterns of behaviour in your relationship that seem to be negative. It helps to put yourself in the other person's shoes when you are talking. Acknowledging your partner's position is not the same as agreeing with it, and sometimes recognizing what they feel about a situation is far more important for the health of your relationship than reaching agreement about the issue. The more you can understand what causes either or both of you to react in a certain way, the better.

After you have talked about an issue, you can then both agree to do things differently. If one person feels that the main responsibility for changing falls on their shoulders, the other can agree ways of helping.

If you are experiencing regular and serious breakdowns in your relationship, talking to your partner may not be possible, so you need to get help from Relate or a family therapist or counsellor (see page 214).

It may be that your relationship has run its course and that you simply need to go your separate ways. While some people see this as failure, I do not. Sometimes one of you has simply changed so much from the person you were when you first got together that moving on becomes the wiser, if painful, course of action.

It is salutary to note that marriages full of anger, hate and disharmony can be more damaging to children than divorce.

Renewing your relationship

Negativity does not have to be the end your relationship. Perhaps it is simply in need of renewal. Some couples go so far as to renew their marital vows in middle age as a way of reconfirming their commitment to each other in front of other people. But the concept of renewal that I have in mind is less dramatic than this and is not aimed just at couples. It is an important aspect of any relationship in a family.

It is all too easy to take someone for granted. After a while we slip into patterns of behaviour and grow accustomed to doing things a certain way. This is especially true of families. While we may not be creating any negative cycles of behaviour, we may be gradually becoming stale.

Taking a break, doing something special, learning something new together – these are just three practical ways in which you might be able to renew a relationship that matters to you.

How can I renew a relationship?

Use the questions below to prompt you into thinking about how you could renew one of your important relationships.

- What does the other person really enjoy doing?
- What do you really enjoy doing together?
- Can you find a time to have a special meal together? If so, where and when?
- Can you plan a trip together? If so, where would you like to go and what will you need to do to make this happen?
- Are there any games you enjoy playing together?
- Do you have favourite films that you both enjoy watching?

Principle 5: Show respect

What is respect? Something to do with being held in high regard? Being admired? Being loved? The answer is probably a combination of all these things and more.

We all need to feel respected. In fact, we seek out relationships in which the other person has a positive image of us as capable, worthy and lovable – in short, worthy of their respect.

Respect is in many ways the bedrock on which effective relationships are built. For where there is respect there is also trust. And where you feel respected you feel valued.

It can be no accident that many of the world's great religions encourage respect of a wife or husband and of certain other key figures among family and close friends. As St Paul puts it in his Letter to the Ephesians (Eph. 4:29): 'Do not let any unwholesome talk come out of your mouths, but only what is helpful for building others up according to their needs, that it may benefit those who listen.'

Introducing respect

While respect is a well-established concept, it is not always easy to see what you can do to turn it into reality in your relationship. Here are some ideas.

1. Think about your partner or someone who is special to you in your family. What are their qualities? Make a list of them.
2. If you have not recently managed to tell your special person what you admire in them, make an opportunity to do so. Thereafter, try to tell them regularly.
3. Look for the positive. Take every opportunity to notice it, offer praise and say nice things.
4. Avoid criticizing.
5. Actively seek small ways to make other family members feel valued and appreciated. A spontaneous hug, or a text message, or a note in a lunch-box reminding someone how much you love and value them can work wonders for their self-esteem and is likely to promote bonding, trust and security.

Making and maintaining close relationships takes an enormous amount of time and energy. There is simply no substitute for these two commodities. But, with luck, the five principles in this chapter will help you to make sure that your efforts are likely to be rewarded.

Troubleshooting

Here are some frequent relationship problems. As always, the answers are signposts for possible action, not hard and fast rules.

I am not getting on with my children.

Conflict is quite normal in families. Since one of your key parental functions is to handle discipline, it may help if you get used to the fact that you are never going to be universally popular! If your children are adolescents or toddlers, some would argue that fostering conflict with you is part of the process by which they learn to separate from you, holding you emotionally at arm's length from time to time.

If the conflict is enduring and you really feel that your relationship with your children is deteriorating, the first thing to do is sit down together and talk openly with them about the situation and acknowledge your feelings about it. You might also want to check out how you would feel if you were on the receiving end of the treatment you mete out, and consider whether your expectations of your children are realistic.

It is easy to forget that the same rules apply to relationships with children as to any other relationship. Respectful and positive attitudes on both sides are necessary if the relationship is to flourish.

I am not sure I like my child.

Again, reassure yourself that it is perfectly normal to go through phases of disliking your child, especially if his behaviour is irritating, so don't beat yourself up about it. You cannot help what you feel, but you are responsible for your actions towards your child, so don't let your temporary feeling of dislike feed into punitive or dismissive treatment.

Try to identify any specific causes for your feelings and see whether you can find ways to address them with your child. Perhaps you dislike him because he is currently making you feel bad about yourself: maybe his attitude is making you feel like a useless parent.

The temptation when you feel like this is to spend as little time as possible with your child, but this is precisely the time when you need to be making the effort to spend constructive time together. Look through the photo albums and remind yourself of qualities in your child that have previously made you warm to him.

You could create new opportunities to allow him to demonstrate those characteristics, but also recognize that he is growing and developing and that you might need to get to know each other afresh (see page 70).

As a single parent, I find it impossible to make a new relationship.

It's certainly not easy to be a single parent, but remember that statistically there are lots of others out there in the same boat. Also, don't just assume that the fact you have children already will be off-putting to potential partners. That is not the case, and anyway, presumably you wouldn't want to be with someone who wasn't going to feel positive about your children as well.

You could try joining one of the single-parent support networks (see page 214), but if you do want to find a new relationship, it may help if you think practically about how you can organize your life and childcare in a way that will enable you to meet prospective partners.

Get yourself a reliable babysitter and consider your options: speed-dating, dining clubs and a reputable introduction agency are all perfectly legitimate ways to meet new people. As a final thought, ask yourself whether there is anyone you already know who might be interested in a date with you. Sometimes the right person can be under your nose without your realizing it.

My child says that she hates my new partner.

This is quite normal, particularly if your child feels that bonding with the newcomer is disloyal to an absent parent. Remember that you, not your child, chose the new partner, and that she is under no obligation to feel the same way about the partner as you do.

If you have been single for a while, your child might also resent the new partner for taking you away from her after a period during which she has had your undivided attention. Try to acknowledge your child's feelings and her right to have them, but also make clear that you expect her to behave in a respectful and civil way towards the new partner.

Explain that the person is not a replacement for her absent parent and that you would like her at least to try getting to know the new partner properly before writing him or her off. Make sure that your new partner is not doing anything to aggravate the situation. You might like to request that in the early stages of the relationship all matters of discipline are referred back to you so the partner does not appear to be immediately assuming a parental role.

Keep talking to your child about her feelings and give it time.

Moving on

In this chapter we have taken the lid off some of the tough issues in relationships, and need to bear in mind the words of author Leo Buscaglia: 'Don't smother each other. No one can grow in the shade'.

In the next chapter we move on to the controversial area of love. What is it? Why is it important? How can you stay in love with another partner (if you choose to) once all the other demands of family life make their presence felt?

CHAPTER **4** Staying in Love

Love is a condition in which the happiness of another person is essential to your own.

Robert Heinlein, author (1907–88)

For some people there is an almost inevitable likelihood that as their relationship changes, they will somehow fall out of love. Are you one of these people? Or are you committed to the idea of being in different kinds of love with a close partner for a lifetime? Take a moment to review these questions.

- How well do you know your partner and their needs?
- Where did you meet and what first attracted you to each other?
- What do you admire about your partner?
- How often do you spend time together?
- What would you like your partner to do differently?
- What problems are you currently facing?
- How has your relationship changed so far?
- How do you imagine your relationship is likely to change over the coming years?

First of all, if you are reading this chapter and are (a) unhappily single, (b) contentedly single, or (c) fed up with the general emphasis on coupledom in contemporary society, please forgive me for presuming that you have a partner with whom you may want to stay in love. Being single and being in a couple are both realistic life choices in which great happiness is possible, but if you would rather not hear about coupledom, I suggest you skip the next few pages.

This chapter is here because for the majority of people, rightly or wrongly, the love relationship with another adult is incredibly important to their happiness, their view of the world, and to how they bring up children.

Conforming to type

There is huge pressure on us to be successful. Along with this there is pressure to conform to what the media portray as happiness in love. We are constantly served up with a stream of idealized images that can easily lead us to assume that there is a template for a perfect relationship. We are continually invited to compare ourselves with other people, who often seem to have better bodies, more fashionable clothes and more exciting lives. No wonder we feel short-changed.

There is no template for being happy in love. What works for you is what is right. All this chapter seeks to do is offer a few principles that might help you to work out your own formula.

Types of love

Canadian sociologist John Lee suggests that there are six different types of love.

Passionate: This type of love focuses on beauty and physical attractiveness. Passionate lovers tend to feel sensual and to need such feelings to be returned. They like touch, believe in love at first sight and are sensitive about their looks.

Game-playing: This is a variation of romantic love, with the lover seeing it as a game. Game-players flirt a lot and often keep their partner guessing about how committed they are. They end relationships when they stop being fun, and tend to get over them quickly.

Friendship: This type of love involves as much caring as passion. Friendship lovers often say that their love is based on shared interests and tastes. They can earn this kind of love and are unlikely to 'fall' into it.

Pragmatic: This type of love is practical and rational. Pragmatic lovers believe in making a relationship work. They are likely to be interested in their partner's parenting and earning powers, and impressed by their career and possessions.

Possessive: This an extreme form of romantic love. Possessives are uncertain and anxious about their relationships. They get jealous easily, and may harm themselves to get their partner's attention if they are ignored.

Selfless: This kind of love involves giving and compassion, and may well include a religious component. Selfless lovers tend to believe that they can use their strengths to help their partner through difficult periods.

Where do you fit?

In light of the six types of love just described, take a moment to think about you and your partner, then answer the following questions.

▶ Which type of lover do you think you are now?
▶ And what type of lover is your partner?

Many relationships start out as romantic love, but become more pragmatic as they develop. In fact, most relationships change their nature over time. While no single type of love is the ideal, a combination of altruism, pragmatism and passion has much to commend it.

Problems tend to arise when partners have different expectations or approaches. For example, a possessive lover may well get hurt by a game-playing one, while a passionate lover may not be satisfied with someone who is content to be pragmatic about the relationship.

It helps to be honest with yourself and your partner about what you think is going on. Just talking about it is useful. Ask your partner what you might do as a lover that you are not doing now. Then reverse roles. While it is often not possible to satisfy all your partner's 'demands', at least you are beginning to talk openly about them.

What about sex?

Ask the question 'To what extent are sex and love part of the same picture?' and you will get many different answers. On the spectrum from celibacy to partner swapping, the majority will be somewhere in the middle and will see sexual fidelity as a cornerstone of their relationship.

Sex is a particularly complex area to explore neutrally when so much of what we see in the media suggests a sexual motive for almost every action. This dilemma is most acute for young people, just at the time when they are exploring their own personality and sexuality. Indeed, they are likely to assume that relationships are all about sexual attraction and sex itself.

What do you think about sex?

Consider the following questions and pause for thought before you answer.

- Can you be in love with someone but not have (or want) sex with them?
- Is it possible to have a loving marriage or partnership with someone without sex?
- Is it possible to be happy with someone whose sexual needs are very different from your own?
- How strong do you consider your own sexual needs to be?
- What is a normal amount of sex for you? Has it changed or remained broadly similar in your life to date? Can you account for this?

Questions like these have been debated by experts and ordinary people over centuries, and there are no right or wrong answers. However, there are some things that we are learning about this complex area.

- A really close adult loving relationship tends to involve some element of sex.
- For adults who are in love, sex is a wonderful way of exploring and deepening their loving relationship.
- Sex on its own is unlikely to make a loving relationship.
- You can get better, more confident and more open about sex with a loving partner.
- When sex is going well between two people, it is a positive and integral part of a loving relationship, but still only a small part of it.
- When couples have problems with sex, the issue can become incredibly powerful and dominating.
- Sexual love may wane, but emotional love grows (and you can work on this aspect of your relationship).

The key to many of the questions that arise in relationships is the ability to be open with your partner and talk freely, making sure that you listen out for your partner's views and needs.

Of course, it's tough to remember to focus on staying in love with your partner when you are also working hard at being a parent and there's a 'third person' in the bed. This third person can literally be a child, but it can also be an abstract (namely, the marriage or the relationship itself), which seems to extend a heavy hand over a couple's continuing interest in sexual exploration.

But whether or not you have children, all relationships change. What might once have felt marvellously fresh and exciting can later seem ordinary, even dull.

Keeping the passion alive

How do you keep your sex life going when juggling the demands of family life? It's not easy. You may simply have to accept the constraints when your children are young, but having the right mindset will help. If you stop comparing what you are currently able to achieve with the glorious heights of your past sexual achievements and start valuing the idea of 'good enough', you are more likely to find contentment. Any sex that you can achieve is a nod in the right direction. It can be valued and celebrated even though it falls short of the ideal.

Parents' complaints about sex

The most common complaints among parents after the arrival of children are:

- Spontaneity is gone.
- You're always rushed.
- There are endless interruptions.
- You cannot explore.
- There's no privacy.
- You can never quite relax.
- You are always too tired.
- Too many 'quickies' are unsatisfying.

All of these (and more) are true. That's why, if you have young children, it's probably better to lower your expectations for your sex life. With a bit of luck, you will be overflowing with happiness in other areas and this may compensate a bit.

Ringing the changes

Whatever stage your relationship is at, variety, adventure and spontaneity are important elements of loving sex. It's so easy to get stuck in a rut sexually, especially when our culture is so quick to hand out roles and expectations in the form of gender stereotypes. Nowhere is this more evident than in the realm of sex. Take the old chestnut regarding the man's role as sexual initiator. Interestingly, in a recent survey, 64 per cent of men said that they wanted their female partner to be more proactive in initiating sex.

There are no rules. It's your relationship and what works for you as a couple is what counts. This is particularly important when it comes to the frequency of sexual activity. Figures vary, but about 60–70 per cent of people say that they have sex 2–3 times a week. Then there is the old cliché that men tend to want more sex. Again, it's worth noting that another recent survey showed that although 68 per cent of men wanted more sex, so did 40 per cent of the women interviewed.

You also need to be aware that what works for the other person may be different from what works for you. Part of the thrill and the challenge is cracking the erotic code of your particular relationship.

Did you know?

- 39 per cent of men say they want more oral sex, whereas 45 per cent of women want their partner to explore all parts of their body.
- 27 per cent of women say that they would be more readily aroused if their partners spent more time talking about important issues in the relationship and cuddled them more.

So take your time, but also be prepared to grab opportunities when you can. Spontaneity is important as the realities of family life may limit the chance for extended bouts of passion. Instead, look for opportunities to fit in a 'quickie'.

Having said that, sometimes it is important to plan ahead so that you can devote time to nurturing the erotic side of your relationship. Sex doesn't have to be a marathon, but when men and women say they want sex to last longer, what they really mean to say is that they want foreplay to last longer.

Like anything else in your life, if sex is important to you, make it a priority. Schedule it in if necessary. This way you are at least likely to enjoy the thrill of anticipation. Just because you have set time aside doesn't mean that you can't preserve a spirit of adventure. In fact, the reverse is often true.

Dare to share

Some people are brought up to think that all talk about sex is dirty. Not true! It can be one of the most loving and erotic aspects of a relationship. Appreciate that sharing your fantasies is an act of intimacy.

It is important to recognize that people may be excited about things in fantasy that they would never consider (or enjoy) if they were happening in real life. This is fine. It will help you if you create a climate in which it feels safe for your partner to share with you what he or she fantasizes about. This means that you must resist the urge to judge, moralize or mock. Your partner is taking a risk sharing these intimate thoughts with you, and this needs to be respected, honoured and maybe even reciprocated.

What's your fantasy?

The chances are that your partner has a whole raft of sexual fantasy that he or she has never disclosed to you.

▷ Try it out. Share some of your most private fantasies with someone you love.

And remember, when you do try out new things, you may need to do them more than once before you can decide as a couple whether this is something that you want to integrate into your sexual repertoire. Too often couples try something once, but never revisit or familiarise themselves with a new source of pleasure or intimacy.

Provided one of you does not find the new experience so off-putting that you have no wish to repeat it, you may like to give yourself a chance to keep going until you have proved to your satisfaction that you either do (or don't) like it. All the while it is essential to keep talking about what you do and don't like. And if you are pursuing more extreme forms of sex, you may need to have a safety 'stop' signal agreed beforehand. No one can read your mind, so your partner needs feedback about what is working for you.

Love is a many-splendoured thing

The most important fact about love is that it takes many forms. Not only are there several types of love, but there are also different kinds of love relationships – heterosexual, homosexual and bisexual.

While there are no precise data about the numbers of gay men and women in the UK, the National Survey of Sexual Attitudes and Lifestyles undertaken in 1989–90 and again in 1999–2000 provides some useful information. It involved 19,000 interviewees and showed a steady increase in the number of men and women who reported same-sex experiences. The greatest change was the increase in women who indicated that they had had a same-sex sexual experience.

If you look at same-sex sexual attraction rather than sexual experience, the figures have also changed over the ten-year period, with women showing the most significant difference. In 1990 some 93.3 per cent of men said they had only ever felt sexual attraction towards the opposite sex, but by 2000 this had fallen to 91.9 per cent. Among the women in 1990 some 93.6 per cent said they had only ever been attracted to men, but by 2000 this had dropped to 88.3 per cent. From this we can therefore deduce that 11.7 per cent of women and 8.1 per cent of men have felt a sexual attraction towards the same sex at least once in their life.

These figures are by no means meant to imply that love is simply about sex or sexual attraction. It's just the way the data is presented in this survey.

Five principles to help you stay in love

The spark that attracts us to someone may be entirely spontaneous, but maintaining it requires some conscious effort. Here are five principles you can apply to your relationship.

Principle 1: Know your partner

The importance of self-knowledge and an understanding of those close to you has already been discussed in general terms (see page 55), but these things are especially important when it comes to your partner.

When you first meet someone, it is obvious that you will want to find out more about them. Indeed, this is part of the fun of the 'chase'. But once you have discovered the most obvious things, it is easy to allow your curiosity to lapse.

To keep love alive it is important to keep your relationship fresh and keep rediscovering each other. When you fall in love, you suddenly learn new things about your partner's interests. Once you know what your partner really enjoys doing, you can show your love by doing them together, or, if this is more helpful, by making it possible for your partner to do them (perhaps by looking after the children). As you grow older together, research suggests that couples can keep the passion going by engaging in novel and challenging activities. This way you are likely to continue to learn new things about each other and to enjoy shared challenges.

One of the most important aspects of knowing your partner is the recognition that people have an innate tendency to grow, evolve and change over time. Change can be experienced as a threat or as a stimulating opportunity to explore new aspects of your 'other half'. If your relationship accommodates this change, it can be mutually enriching. The more you can actively allow each other to grow, supporting each other in the pursuit of personal dreams and interests, the better for both of you. Happy, fulfilled individuals are likely to make better partners and better lovers.

When you explored your knowledge of those close to you on page 55, the questions focused on what you know about their likes and dislikes. They also touched on the ways in which you choose to organize your domestic life.

But what really matters are the emotional things – the degree to which you understand the emotional toing and froing between you. How aware are you of what makes your partner happy or sad? How does your partner express his or her emotions? And how does this make you feel? To what extent are you prepared to be really honest about your own feelings with your partner? Do either of you tend to express your feelings in ways that are unhelpful or destructive to the relationship? What happens when one of you is at a really low ebb? Do you manage to deal with such situations in ways that are respectful of each other, or do you end up shouting or sulking?

The answers to these questions (and your willingness to talk about these issues openly) are what I am getting at here.

As you come to know more about your partner, you need to keep growing as a person too. In fact, all the while you are with someone you are changing. The more you can be discovering what is best and most exciting in yourself, the more you will be confident to explore your partner.

It's a paradox of being in love that although you might think it would be desirable to get closer and closer to your partner, becoming too close can turn into dependency and ultimately destroy love. If you rely too much on someone else and start to seem needy yourself, you inevitably become less attractive. In some sense, therefore, while you get to know your partner and he or she gets to know you, it may be helpful to keep a little bit of independence too.

In addition, independence is important in case your relationship goes wrong or you suddenly find yourself on your own. In these circumstances it allows you still to be the 'full' you. If you can approach your relationship in this spirit, you are likely to value your differences and not see them as a source of conflict.

Marks and Spencer plc
Waterside House
35 North Wharf Road
London W2 1NW

Mixed Sources
Product group from well-managed
forests and other controlled sources
www.fsc.org Cert no.SGS-COC-005999
© 1996 Forest Stewardship Council

This receipt is made from FSC certified paper, part of our
Plan A commitment to use more sustainable materials.

FSC, protecting the world's forests for the future.

www.marksandspencer.com

Marks and Spencer plc
Waterside House
35 North Wharf Road
London W2 1NW

Mixed Sources
Product group from well-managed
forests and other controlled sources
www.fsc.org Cert no.SGS-COC-005999
© 1996 Forest Stewardship Council

This receipt is made from FSC certified paper, part of our
Plan A commitment to use more sustainable materials.

FSC, protecting the world's forests for the future.

MARKS & SPENCER

123 High Street
Bromley
BR1 1JL
020 8460 9131
VAT NO. GB232128892

£

09419735T54 JODPHUR TRS	15.00R
05260300T54 OPP CORD	9.00R
01944952T01 CASHMILLON GLOVES	3.00R

Items: 3   Balance to Pay   **27.00**

Gift Card Tendered   27.00

Thank you for shopping at M&S
Please retain for your records

Last day for a full refund or exchange
03/02/2011
After this you may be entitled to
a refund in line with your legal rights

PLEASE RETAIN FOR YOUR RECORDS

30/12/10   15:56   08045355 11918   136 0903

9 990209031360119188

Principle 2: Nurture, affirm and admire

Love grows when you help your partner to grow (nurture), constantly confirm their strengths (affirm) and actively praise (admire) them for who they are. Perhaps these and other characteristics of love help to explain why so many people find comfort in this extract from St Paul's Letter to the Corinthians (I Cor. 13:4).

> *Love is patient, love is kind.*
> *It does not envy, it does not boast, it is not proud.*
> *It is not rude, it is not self-seeking.*
> *It is not easily angered, it keeps no record of wrongs.*
> *Love does not delight in evil, but rejoices with the truth.*
> *It always protects, always trusts, always hopes, always perseveres.*
> *Love never fails.*

As you read these positive words, perhaps you are thinking that they are all too obvious, even simplistic. Of course you need to do all this stuff! But it is surprising how easy it is to stop doing it. Familiarity breeds forgetfulness. It may be that all you have to do is become a little more conscious of the importance of these words. Or perhaps your relationship is not as good as it once was, and one or both of you has become a little forgetful.

You may find it reassuring to know that research suggests there is a strong connection between happy relationships and the amount of positive 'stroking' couples give each other.

At the heart of this principle is generosity. As Mahatma Gandhi (1869–1948) once put it: 'We must become the change we want to see'. When you become more loving, your partner experiences this and is, in turn, more likely to want to reciprocate.

If you celebrate the best in your partner, not only do you make them feel better about themselves, but you are also giving them something to live up to.

The flip side of this coin is the need to avoid various corrosive negative approaches. These include:

- Dwelling on the past
- Making too much of faults
- Using sarcasm
- Using put-downs.

Each of these approaches eats away at love like acid on metal.

Are you self-aware?

If you are feeling strong, spend a moment thinking about times when you have found yourself using any of the negative approaches listed at the bottom of page 83.

Remember, being self-aware is the first step to changing your behaviour.

The desired situation in a loving relationship is that you help each other play to your strengths. By deliberately exploring each other's strengths and weaknesses, you can determine those areas in which you take the lead, where you play support roles and where a role is shared. Rather than relying on gender stereotypes, this process is likely to help you make the best of your partner's individual skills and abilities, and minimize destructive forms of competition.

What this means is that rather than focusing on the faults of the other person, you try to understand your own reactions and seek ways in which you might need to change.

Cultivate trust

For love to flourish it is essential that there is trust between you. Not only do you need to be turned on by your partner, you also need to feel emotionally safe with them. This means having the courage to be open about what is going on inside, even if you feel this might mean disclosing feelings or facts that the other person is not going to like.

It is in the nature of human relationships that in small ways, and sometimes in big ways, we all violate trust at some point. We say or do something, perhaps without thinking it through, and cause pain to a loved one. What matters most as far as the long-term health and survival of the relationship are concerned is how these breaches of faith are managed and how honestly and sincerely they are repaired.

It is a great tragedy that anger and hurt can cause people to destroy perfectly viable relationships. The key to survival is to keep talking. Sometimes trust is violated because people are not able to disclose what is going on. They then act it out in the form of a more destructive behaviour, perhaps by having an affair or developing an addiction.

The bottom line here is the need to treat each other with respect. It's very easy for couples to become over-familiar with one another. As part of showing someone respect, it is helpful if you actively appreciate those qualities that you admire in them. As Mark Twain once said, 'I can live for two months on a good compliment.' Now there's a salutary reminder to go off and find something nice to say about your partner right now.

How to nurture, affirm and admire the person you love

1. Make a list of all the things you admire about your partner (or, if you are going through a bad patch, all the things you used to admire). Over the period of a week try to tell your partner as many of these things as you can. Or, if the moment seems right and you are alone together, tell them as many things as you can in one go.

2. Don't forget that it matters when and how you do this. If you appear to be using some kind of formula that your heart isn't in, it will not have the desired effect.

3. Notice when your partner shows off the qualities that you admire and remark on it. 'I really liked the way that…' 'You are so good at…' 'That was typically kind of you to…'

4. Make sure you have an up-to-date photo of your partner and the two of you together in your wallet and at work. Use these as a prompt to think about what your partner may be feeling at any particular moment.

5. Give your partner something that you know they will think is special. And give it to them not on a birthday or anniversary, but on an ordinary day. This will show a bit of your affection and thoughtfulness. However, avoid gifts that may have the opposite effect, such as a bunch of drooping flowers bought in guilty haste from a garage forecourt. These give out a message not of love, but of your inability to prioritize your love.

6. Make an effort to give your partner a hug and tell them that you love them. Your knowledge of them will help to ensure that you pick a good time, not a moment when they are preoccupied or distracted.

7. Make sure you know which music your partner really enjoys, and build up a collection of it. Or if your partner actually prefers peace and quiet, turn off your own music from time to time.

8. Say 'thank you'. We all like to be appreciated, and articulating it helps to maintain a loving relationship and ensure that it does not go stale.

We've got this gift of love, but love is like a precious plant. You can't just accept it and leave it in the cupboard or just think it's going to get on by itself. You've got to keep watering it; really look after it and nurture it.

John Lennon, singer/songwriter (1940–80)

Principle 3: Spend time together

How much time do you spend with your partner in a typical working week? Do you pass by each other like ships in the night? If you do manage to spend time together, do you find yourself flopping in front of the television? Or do you manage to spend at least one evening doing something together that allows you to chat about more than administrative matters, such as who will take the car in for servicing? (See Chapter 7 for ideas.)

The surest signal of love that you can give someone is to spend time with them of your own free will. Choosing to spend time with someone tells them that you think they are special and important. By contrast, if you are always too busy, or work always takes precedence, or the children always seem to have more pressing needs, your partner will inevitably pick up a message that you are not really interested. If someone does not feel wanted, it is easy for love to evaporate.

In the early days of a relationship, when there is a hunger partly driven by sexual attraction and the thrill of the new, it is easy. But after a few years it can become more challenging. If you want to stay in love, you need to prioritize your relationship. This is not about 'working at it' in a laboured, effortful sense, but about protecting your relationship from the pressures of everyday life and giving it space to grow and develop. As you do so, it should become intrinsically rewarding and you will want to spend more time, rather than less, cultivating it. And when you spend time together it is much more likely that you will talk about things that really matter. You will begin to understand more about what motivates you spiritually, about each other's deepest hopes and fears, about your families.

With busy lives, you may need to be creative about how to ensure that you have time together, and equally creative when choosing how to spend that time. How you use it to explore and enjoy each other will depend on your individual personalities. Sometimes it is important just to listen to your partner without interrupting.

Great ways to spend time together

1. Make a date. Treat it just like making an appointment for anything else in your life.

2. Deal with the practical stuff separately. All families have to make plans for the week ahead – who's going where, lifts, school trips, shopping, etc. This can all too easily become the only kind of time you spend together. Before, during or after supper on a Sunday works for many people. But the important thing is to decide on a time that is good for you.

3. Plan to do different kinds of things together. Walking, love-making, shopping for an important household item, planning a holiday, working through a difficult issue – all these and more are the kind of things you might want to do.

4. Turn off the phones. If you have children, tell them that this is your special time together and teach them to interrupt you only in a dire emergency. (Spell out what this might be.)

5. Find a place you like to be. It might be a different place at different times of the year. It can become 'your' place, somewhere you particularly enjoy being together.

6. Talk about what you *want* to talk about (as opposed all the household administration that can so easily dominate conversation).

7. Be realistic. Even if you manage to spend only twenty minutes together to begin with, this is still progress if you were failing to spend any good time together before.

Principle 4: Develop your own language

Ever heard of the word 'idiolect'? It means your own personal language: the way you (and no one else) use words. The first time I heard this term I fell in love with it. It provided an excuse for all the silly things that I say and have said over the decades.

When I was a child, my sister and I created a language that went something like this: 'Igadi wagadant togadoo playgaday nowgadow.' (I want to play now.) Can you see the rule that makes this strange language work? (You put all or part of 'agada', depending on the preceding vowel sound, into every syllable of each word.) The point of our language was that whereas my parents spoke a pseudo-French when they wanted to exclude us from their conversation, this was how my sister and I communicated to keep adults out. It was part of our idiolect as siblings.

Language is a vital part of love-making and of staying in love. And developing your own private ways of communicating with each other is a key aspect of developing a shared intimacy. Don't get me wrong. I am not suggesting that you should go around speaking a silly language to feel happy.

But perhaps you have pet names for each other. This suggests that you feel completely safe together. You are choosing to let down your guard and be playfully vulnerable with another person (because these terms may well sound ridiculous to anyone else who hears them). Private terms of endearment can become part of a messaging system between you, a kind of code – your personal idiolect.

What's your idiolect?

▶ Do you have special names for your partner? Have they been the same for a long time?

▶ Do some words have particular meanings in your relationship or in your family?

Of course, developing a shared intimacy is a far bigger issue than the linguistics it might involve. It's not just what you say that matters, but how and when you say it. There is generous language and there are words that blame, criticize and are generally negative. Listen out for the kind of language you and your partner are using, and try to avoid negative ways of speaking because these rapidly corrode love. Contrary to the playground rhyme 'Sticks and stones may break my bones but words will never hurt me', words are powerful and can cause real hurt in a relationship.

To a certain extent, staying in touch is the simplest and easiest form of comfort. Some people like to go to work and not communicate with their loved one or family until they walk through the front door again at the end of the day. Sometimes this is inevitable; very busy days leave no space for shared intimate moments while at work. But in most people's working life there are moments here and there. Simply calling and briefly asking your partner how it's going, especially when you know they are having a tough time, can be extremely supportive and a good way of showing your love. You may not be able to offer any practical help, but you are demonstrating that you are thinking about them. And if you can, choose the right moment for your partner to receive your call, showing them that you remember when they are likely to be free enough to respond.

Keep in touch

Here are some ideas for keeping the lines of communication open when you are apart.

1. Make it a habit to call your partner at least once during the day to ask how they are doing.

2. If you and your partner are having a busy day, make sure you leave a voicemail. Tell them that you are thinking about them and that you love them.

3. If you are leaving early and will not overlap at breakfast, leave a nice note for your partner to find during the day.

4. Text a message using your own personal terms of endearment.

5. Don't restrict yourself to messages or notes: talk to your partner face to face and tell them directly about your love for them.

There are two aspects of your shared language that it is interesting to examine: which person you use ('I/we' or 'you' or 'he/she/they') and your choice of tone when making suggestions.

Generally speaking, it is helpful if you can develop a way of talking that uses either the first person singular ('*I* really think we should do something about those curtains') or first person plural ('*We* really enjoy going on walking holidays'). The singular form is effective when you are trying to explain what you think or feel. But the plural form is potentially the most useful for helping to ensure your love endures because 'we' suggests that you are acting jointly and in harmony. There is one important caveat: do not assume your partner's opinion and use the plural 'we' when it might be better sticking to the singular 'I'.

Compare this with couples who talk about each other in the third person: 'He never gets home before seven o'clock' or 'She always seems to prefer it when I wear these shoes'. The third person can be impersonal or downright critical. It seems detached. Listen out for the times when you use it. Of course, it is a perfectly useful way of sharing practical information – 'John will be back early tonight' – especially when you use a name to personalize it.

Sometimes it's necessary to use 'you'. When you need help or want to give advice, for example, it is the obvious choice of person. But look at the following two statements:

> 'When you clean those glasses, you must hold them gently by the stem.'

'When you clean those glasses, you might like to hold them really carefully by the stem. They're so fragile.'

Most people prefer the tone of the second statement. The use of 'might' rather than 'must' is respectful and leaves plenty of opportunity for interpretation. 'Must' is bossy and makes assumptions that there is only one way.

Language really matters. Notice the way your friends talk to each other and see what you can deduce about ways of talking that seem more loving than others.

Of course, language does not have to be verbal. From the moment we are born, we need physical touch, and this is a key part of communicating within a loving relationship. The language of touch has many dialects. There is the reassuring touch upon your shoulder, the comfort of a hug, the togetherness of holding hands, the intimacy of sexual foreplay... Touch is an extremely subtle and powerful language. While it can be intensely erotic, it need not be. In fact, learning (or relearning) the art of regular non-sexual touch is a key element of expressing love.

A good way of ensuring that there is plenty of touch in your relationship is to give each other massages on a regular or occasional basis. You could start by having individual massages from a professional so that you get better at saying what you like. Then you might like to take a class together and actually learn how to do it properly. Or maybe you just prefer trial and error and learning as you go along.

What's your pleasure?

▶ Take time to ask each other how you like to be touched, then practise the techniques.

Principle 5: Recognize and tackle problems together

All relationships have problems or challenges, but some seem to have more than their fair share. Some couples see problems as things to be overcome together. Others prefer to blame each other, get angry or simply ignore them, as if they might go away of their own accord.

If you want to stay happily in love, you really have no choice but to recognize and tackle problems together.

Start from a basis of fairness

Ideally, you should see if you can be a couple who seem to have fewer than their fair share of problems. This can be greatly helped by ensuring that you share everything in a way that seems fair to you both. For example, sharing out the household chores may be particularly important to one partner (see more on this in Chapter 7), but the other might consider being home at a predictable hour to help put the children to bed much more helpful. Similarly, money might be the issue for one person, but how you spend time together may be more important to the other.

If your relationships is one in which you both think things are generally fair, you are likely to find tackling problems much easier.

What's the matter?

▷ Take a moment to think about all the things in your relationship that really matter to you and that, if they go wrong, cause problems. Use the words below to prompt you, then think of some more of your own:

access to children, birthdays, chores, children, clothes, emotion,

ex-partner, friends, gifts, jealousy, love-making, money,

personalities, relatives, sleeping, step-children, time, work

▷ If you know each other well, you probably already know a bit about your views for each item on your list. Do any of the things you have listed currently cause major differences of opinion? Honestly examine and share your feelings about any differences. What expectations do you each have? What are your assumptions? Are there any unfairnesses? If you find things that are unfair, can you commit to rectifying them?

Notice problems

Let's assume that you are both relatively content with the way things are currently shared. The next step is to be able to spot things happening that feel wrong to you before they become serious.

There are two aspects to noticing. The first requires you and your partner to be honest and open about what is going on. The second involves being clearer about the nature of the issue you are facing.

John Gottman's research suggests that problems in relationships divide into two categories: those that can be solved and those that he describes as 'perpetual'. Solvable problems are often related to specific situations, such as conflict over whether you should go to a film together or visit your partner's family for supper. Perpetual problems tend to relate to underlying personality types – the way you express emotions, or whether you like to leave things to the last minute or prepare well in advance. 'Perpetual' issues are, inevitably, more difficult to get to grips with.

It is perfectly possible to have a happy relationship that has both solvable and perpetual problems. Indeed, most of us are in this situation. But if you have too many of either type of problem, one or both of you is likely to feel anger, resentment and unhappiness. Something that starts out as a relatively small, solvable habit – the way one of you leaves a mess in the bathroom, for example – can escalate into a much bigger issue of how one of you seems not to care how the home is looked after.

If you can notice and talk about problems openly, you have already started on the road to finding a solution.

What's your problem?

▶ Take the list of key areas you produced on page 91. Does it suggest that you and your partner have any specific problems? If so, are they are of the solvable or perpetual type?

Tackle problems in ways that work for you

Problems are inevitable, as is the conflict they create, because life throws up all sorts of challenges that do not necessarily have simple answers. It's how you tackle problems that determines the quality of your relationship and, ultimately, whether it will survive.

How to tackle problems

Here are some general approaches that seem to work.

1. Make sure you understand the other person's point of view. Ask open-ended questions that invite him or her to share information. These tend to start with 'who', 'when', 'what', 'how' or 'where'. Try to avoid 'why' questions, as these tend to produce a more defensive reply. Remember that many problems are simply a cry to be listened to. In fact, just listening properly may ease the anxiety that your partner is feeling.

2. Before you reply, repeat what the other person has said. This will help you to be sure that you have really understood what concerns your partner, as well as demonstrating your respect.

3. Try to keep an open and positive mindset for as long as possible, looking for solutions that will work for you both. This may involve finding common ground between you: 'I can see that we are agreed on x and y, but we still need to sort out z'.

4. Choose an appropriate time to tackle your problems. You both need to be able to devote your energy to working things through, and if one person's mind is elsewhere or they are very tired, it might be better to choose another time.

5. Make clear requests for change. If something is bothering you, say so. For example, 'When you do x, I feel really bad because... Please could you try doing y next time?'

6. Avoid provocative language and critical statements.

7. Try to keep the problem separate from your partner's personality. It's very important that you do not appear to be launching a general offensive on someone's character. So if, for example, one of you prefers to leave things to the last minute, avoid suggesting that this is an example of their uncaring personality, and instead focus on the specific situation: 'Would you mind if we started getting ready to go out fifteen minutes earlier tonight? It would really help me to feel more relaxed.'

8. Look for solutions that work for you both.

9. Keep focused on the problem in hand. Going over old issues is a recipe for disaster.

10. Deal with one problem at a time.

11. Try to keep your sense of humour alive.

Every time you notice and solve a problem with someone you love, you get closer. Your relationship gets stronger and you are 'banking' goodwill for the next problem around the corner. As you work things through together, you also learn more about each other. All in all you are helping to ensure that you are staying in love and living in the real world at the same time.

Troubleshooting

See if the issues below resonate with you and your situation. As always, the answers are signposts for possible action, not hard and fast rules.

My partner doesn't seem to love me any more.

It is very easy for couples who have been together for a while to take each other for granted and to rely too heavily on assumptions about the other person's experience. In particular, it is easy to forget that in order for someone to feel loved, it necessary to demonstrate love in thoughtful, meaningful ways on a daily basis.

If you feel your relationship is growing distant, don't ignore the warning signs. Discuss your concerns with your partner, but also be proactive in demonstrating the kind of behaviour you would like to see more of.

If the relationship is really in trouble or it is proving difficult to get to the bottom of things, a relationship counsellor could be of genuine help (see page 214).

My sex life is virtually non-existent since we had children.

Raising very young children can be a stressful and exhausting business, and stressed and exhausted partners are not always in the mood for love. The physical process of labour and breastfeeding can leave mothers feeling quite battered and bruised, and it is not unusual for couples to take some time to resume an active sex life.

Even when sexual relations are re-established, it is common for the frequency and duration of love-making to be quite restricted. The important thing is not how often you make love, but that both partners feel OK about the situation. Quality rather than quantity should be your motto, but if you are used to extended love-making sessions in front of the fire, be prepared to get used to seizing the opportunity when it presents itself. The pressure of time can be used to your advantage to savour even a brief encounter. Also bear in mind that if intercourse after childbirth is uncomfortable, you can always explore other non-penetrative forms of sexual expression. Take your time and ease your way back into sex gently. Remember that it is supposed to be pleasurable and fun for both of you.

Some men find it hard to deal with the fact that their partner is now a mother, and may even feel emotionally excluded by the new arrival. New mothers may feel less sexually attractive in the aftermath of pregnancy, and hormonal upheaval may mean that their sex drive is low for a while. It is important to be honest with each other about what you are feeling and discuss anything that is a problem for either of you. If problems continue, approach your GP for a referral for psychosexual counselling.

I think my partner is having an affair.

It is much better to be open with your partner about your fears than to bottle them up. You will do far more damage to the relationship by brooding, looking for signs of unfaithfulness and perhaps setting traps for your partner. The very fact that you are considering this last possibility means that there are some real issues in the relationship, even if it turns out that there are other factors contributing to your feelings of insecurity.

Even if your partner is having an affair, this does not necessarily signal the death knell of your relationship unless you want it to. Depending on their nature, affairs can often be understood as a symptom of other unaddressed problems in the relationship.

While usually highly traumatic for all concerned, the discovery of an affair can in some cases prove to be the turning point that allows couples to confront and overcome the longstanding difficulties that have secretly driven them apart.

If you are facing the possibility that your partner has been unfaithful, remind yourself that you can be OK whether you end up with or without your partner, and that however distressed you may be feeling in the short term, you still have the power to create a happy and fulfilled life for yourself.

My partner and I seem to be growing apart.

Often partners feel this when the implicit psychological contract between them is being secretly renegotiated by one of them without the other's knowledge. Maybe expectations are shifting, leaving the other person feeling bemused or bewildered.

Maybe one or both of you is continuing to grow and change in ways that feel alien and unsettling. If the latter is the case, it may be necessary to spend a bit more time together to keep abreast of the changes taking place and to keep your connection in the present alive.

Moving on

The good news is that it's certainly possible to stay and grow in love. But although this happens instinctively for many people, others may find it takes more conscious attention. I hope that some of what you have read will have reached your heart. As the novelist Antoine de Saint-Exupéry (1900–44) reminds us, 'It is only with the heart that one can see rightly; what is essential is invisible to the eye.'

Now let's move on to the chapter at the heart of this book, where we will have a chance to explore the most complex role on the planet a little more – that of being a parent.

CHAPTER **5** The Challenges of Parenthood

If you've never been hated by your child, you've never been a parent.

Bette Davis, actress (1908–89)

Whether you are just starting out with a new baby or have recently become a proud grandparent, the odds are that you are having or have had your fair share of challenges as a parent. Perhaps you have always sailed through each one, effortlessly surfing the inevitable waves of uncertainty and difficulty. Or perhaps you are reading this book now because the challenge seems to be beyond you. Whatever your feelings about your own parenting to date, take a few moments to consider the following questions.

- What makes a good parent?
- What kind of a parent are you?
- How consistent are you?
- How organized are you?
- Do you find it easy to say 'no'?
- Do you enjoy helping your children to learn new things?
- What do you worry about most?
- Do you have stepchildren? If so, how were things when you first started out?
- Do you involve grandparents in your children's life?
- What is your best moment so far as a parent? And your worst?
- How are you getting on as a family at the moment? And what about as a parent?

Being a parent has never been harder than it is today. The world is changing so fast. Technological developments mean that you and your children are likely to holiday abroad, buy things on the Internet from all over the world and watch television or download music at any time of the day or night.

Patterns of work are different too. Jobs for life don't exist these days. In our 24/7 society more and more people have to work what used to be called 'unsociable hours' but are now an inevitable part of employment in certain sectors. And more people have chosen a different path from traditional employment and, like me, work from home, living a portfolio life.

There is a strong chance that you may be, as I am, part of a 'blended' family, where children who do not all share the same biological mother or father live under the same roof. As a step-parent, you may have had to become a parent overnight, suddenly 'acquiring' the children of the man or woman you love. But blended families take different forms. Perhaps your 'blend' is that you are living in a same-sex relationship, or parenting alone, or sharing a parenting role with someone whose culture and religion are different from yours, or bringing up children you have adopted. Maybe you're a grandparent performing a role that is suspiciously close to the parenting one you fulfilled for your own child many years ago.

These are just the more obvious manifestations of the parenting role today, and go some way to demonstrating why being a parent has never been harder than it is right now. However, you can choose to follow certain principles that are grounded on the experience of real people who manage to live their life a little more happily than others seem to do. (These are the principles outlined in each chapter of this book.)

Some things stay the same, though. If you choose (or are forced) to become a parent, it still ranks as one of the most powerful experiences in a lifetime. Nothing will ever be the same again. While you may feel that up to now you have chosen everything in your life, you do not, except in the rarest of adoption circumstances, choose your children. They just come, with bits of you hardwired into them and lots of their own distinctively different and special personal characteristics waiting to burst out and, over time, be shaped by experiences. Undoubtedly the arrival of children is one of the most significant events in the life of a couple. It can be a time of growth or crisis. Either way, it will certainly require adaptation, not least because research suggests that couples spend two-thirds less time alone together than they did before the birth of a child.

Alongside increasingly fluid families created by divorce and alternatives to marriage, there are other changes taking place in society's view of parenting. For example, where yesterday's 'new man' was likely to be someone who could just about hold his own when it came to housework and nappy-changing, today's is more likely to be a stepdad. There is a particular dilemma for women too. Undoubtedly the pressures of career are much greater than previously, and nowadays women are just as likely as men to walk out if a relationship goes wrong. Yet there is a kind of social stigma attached to women who leave their children, even if there is a perfectly adequate father available and willing to look after them. All this raises interesting questions about the nature of the psychological 'contract' we make with our children.

What does it mean to be a parent?

Take a moment to consider the following questions and work out your own views of what it is to be a parent. You might like to share your thoughts with your partner or a close friend.

▶ What are your responsibilities to your children?

▶ How do these change as the children grow older?

▶ What kind of relationship do you want to have with your children in ten years' time?

▶ How can you ensure that you start laying the foundations for that relationship in the present?

▶ How do you balance your responsibility to your children with your responsibility to others, such as your partner or parents?

▶ And what about yourself? Can you imagine a time when your needs will be more powerful than your child's and that you might have to do something to realize them?

▶ If you are trying to ensure the happiness and overall development of your child, and if you are unhappy in your relationship with their mother or father, when does it become 'fair' for you to move on?

These are really tough questions. You may even feel that they are 'loaded' questions (especially the last one, with its assumption that it may sometimes be in the children's interests for their parents not to stay together). You may well have better, and tougher, questions of your own to pose.

There is a sense in which we have to be careful about the nature of our investment in children. For most of us they are going to be central in our life, so there is likely to be considerable vulnerability in the fact that our own happiness is so linked to their well-being. Are you trying to live through your children? Are you so identified with them that you cannot allow them to make choices and be people whom you would not yourself choose to be? Do you encourage them to be fully themselves? Are you overprotecting them? Can you let go enough to allow them to learn from their own experience, even if you think you know what is best for them?

Your children are not your children:
They are the sons and daughters of life's longing for itself.
They come through you but not from you,
And though they are with you yet they belong not to you.

You may give them your love but not your thoughts,
For they have their own thoughts.
You may house their bodies but not their souls,
For their souls dwell in the house of tomorrow, which you cannot
  visit, not even in your dreams.
You may strive to be like them, but seek not to make them like
  you.
For life goes not backward nor tarries with yesterday.

Khalil Gibran, Lebanese mystic and poet (1833–1931)

Being good enough

The pressure on parents to be perfect is intense. In the media we are surrounded by images of happy, successful couples and their beaming children. The same media take pleasure in publishing every detail of celebrity marriages that go wrong. You do not need to be a parent to have picked up the fact that British schools are testing pupils much more than in the past. And this is another source of pressure on parents, who naturally want to do their best for their children. Go into any major bookshop and you will see stacks of self-help books for parents who want to help their children do better in school tests. We have become a very performance-orientated society.

In the face of all this pressure, one concept may be particularly helpful – the 'good enough parent'. Created by psychologist Donald Winnicott, this reminds us that we do not have to be perfect, because children are like plants – they tend to take what they need from the environment, even if it looks inhospitable. Parents can actually decrease their own effectiveness because they get so preoccupied with doing the right thing all the time. We all want to do the best for our children, but we need to trust ourselves to have the resources we need and to trust that our children are sufficiently robust not to be permanently damaged by every little mistake we might make. We need to keep focused on the bigger picture: it is the overall package that counts. Being good enough is a noble goal for any parent.

Personal identity and parenting

Being a parent brings with it many practical challenges. Of these, one of the less obvious, perhaps, is the challenge it presents to your personal identity.

Western culture is individualistic. Our sense of who we are depends largely on the way we look, what we do with our working hours and free time, where we live, who our friends are, what we believe in and our individual achievements. Before the arrival of children we have focused almost entirely on ourselves, investing considerable time and effort in the process. The arrival of children can be devastating to this personal project. Children can feel all-consuming, and the consensus seems to be that one of the things that can get consumed along the way is our own identity.

From a cultural and historical perspective, we British seem quite poorly equipped for family life. While the Victorian middle class effectively invented a rather sentimental idea of childhood, they also propagated the view that children should be 'seen and not heard'. In other words, children should not be allowed to impinge on the ordered world of adults. Nannies were employed to manage the children offstage so that many parents could continue acting out their adult roles.

These days we seem to fall between two opposing views of parenting. On one hand, parents often seem to struggle with the demands of their children, fantasizing about time away from them in which they can recover some sense of themselves independent of their role as parents. On the other hand, perhaps because we feel guilty about such unworthy but natural impulses, we seem to compensate by creating child-centred families in which the needs of adults are largely ignored. This in turn makes us anxious to have time free from the burden of parenthood, so the whole vicious cycle continues.

Other European cultures seem to have a more relaxed attitude towards children, integrating them into a family life where they appear to be better appreciated and enjoyed. The adults seem less anxious to offload their children in order to protect their personal space. As a consequence, bedtimes tend to be much later and children are welcomed into settings (such as restaurants and bars) that are regarded as adult-only in the UK.

The sensible approach is to find what works for you as a family. But as you do so, it may be helpful to remember that there is not just one right way to be a parent. Families have to provide for the needs of all their members, but how that balance is achieved is up to the family concerned. One size does not fit all. This is true of parents, and of children too, as discussed in the next chapter. Some children flourish in conditions where others might struggle. You need to be flexible enough to match your parenting style to the needs of your specific child(ren).

Your twelve parenting roles

I often get asked if there are right or wrong ways for parents to deal with particular situations. If you have followed the drift of *Happy Families* so far, you may not be surprised to learn that I do not believe there are. However, I do think that certain situations tend to respond better to certain approaches, and that it is very easy for parents to get stuck on one way of doing things.

The twelve pairs of ideas for the parent roles that follow were first developed when I produced some training materials with accelerated learning expert Alistair Smith. These were devised as part of the book *Help Your Child to Succeed* (see page 213).

Looking at the research on styles of parenting, it became clear to me that there are various choices that parents are constantly required to make about their parenting style. Do they stay close or do they hang back? Do they coach or do they tell? Do they focus on the big picture or get involved in the detail? I've narrowed down the parent styles to what I consider the twenty-four most important, and from these you make twelve choices.

What's your parenting style?

▶ Have a look at the parent roles on pages 102–13. Start by going through them all without deciding what kind of a parent you tend to be.

▶ Now go back through each pair of choices and see if you can decide on the one that feels like it is closest to your natural parenting style. The pros and cons of each style are indicated by plus and minus signs.

Sometimes you might find it difficult to decide because the choice depends on particular circumstances.

Sometimes, given your personality, you can be pretty sure what to opt for.

Sometimes you simply might not be sure, or not even find the question helpful.

▶ If you get stuck, ask someone who knows you well as a parent to help you.

▶ If you are feeling really bold and your children are old enough, ask them what they think.

Stay close – *I'm right here if you need me.*

Do you like to hover close to your child at all times and feel worried if he is out of your sight?

+ By staying close to your child you are showing your love for him and helping to keep him safe.

– Your child needs to learn for himself and too much support may be unhelpful.

Hang back – *They'll sort it out on their own.*

Are you happy to let your children work things out on their own, provided they are not in any actual danger?

+ By giving your children a bit of freedom you are allowing them to develop the confidence to work things out for themselves and showing that you trust them.

– Being too laid back could mean that you miss chances to help or correct your child.

Optimist – *Everything will be OK.*

Do you assume that everything will be OK and that you can always sort things out?

+ By being positive you are giving a real confidence boost to your children.

− Optimists can be irritating and sometimes unrealistic.

Pessimist – *Things are bound to go wrong.*

Do you always expect the worst, thinking that things are likely to go wrong if they involve your children?

+ By thinking the worst you may already have good back-up plans in place.

− Pessimists can be irritating by dampening down enthusiasm.

Big picture – *Let's see how it works out.*

Do you prefer to think about the big picture, focusing on your goals and not worrying about how you will get there?

+   People who focus on goals normally get there.

–   Without some attention to detail, you may well miss important things.

Detail – *Let's make a plan.*

Do you prefer to plan things in detail, checking out timings, people and places beforehand?

+   By planning well you will create lots of opportunities for your child.

–   You might miss the wood for the trees.

Relaxed – *Let's use the ground-sheet, then it doesn't matter what happens.*

Do you feel relaxed when your kids are playing, and not worry that they will destroy your house?

+　　If you are relaxed, your children will be likely to pick this up.

–　　If you are too relaxed, you may not notice things that are happening.

Anxious – *Let me hold that or you'll spill it.*

Are you constantly worrying that your children will ruin your furniture and harm themselves?

+　　Your house will probably look good.

–　　Your children may not be able to relax if you are always fretting about things.

Fun-loving – *Let's have a good laugh about it.*

Is your natural response to most things to smile? Do you tend to laugh at the things your children get up to?

+   Laughter is a great way of coping with situations and dealing with stress.

−   Sometimes other adults may not share your sense of humour.

Serious – *I'm going to stop this if you don't play properly.*

Do you wish your family would take life more seriously? Do you tend to be frowning when others are laughing?

+   It's helpful to show common sense, especially when others are getting silly.

−   If you are too serious, you may end up giving yourself unnecessary stress.

Like variety – *Let's see what games they know.*

Do you enjoy new experiences, preferring not to know what will happen in any one day?

+ By showing your own interest in new things you are encouraging your child's sense of curiosity.

– While you may be fine, others may find it scary if they do not have at least a rough idea of what they are going to do.

Like routine – *Let's play the same games we did last year.*

Do you feel happier if you are doing things that you have already tried once and feel comfortable with?

+ As you know what you are going to do, it is likely that you will have prepared it well.

– If your children rely too much on things you have planned earlier, they may never learn how to cope with the unexpected.

Show emotions – *Let me give you a big hug.*

Do you naturally tend to show your feelings by hugging those you love? Do you enjoy talking about what you feel?

+ By surrounding your child with such obvious signs of your love you are really helping her to feel secure.

− Sometimes children need space to work out their own emotions rather than deal with yours.

Keep emotions inside – *That was well done.*

Do you prefer to keep your feelings to yourself? Do you find it difficult to show others what you are feeling?

+ There's no right way of dealing with feelings, and many people prefer to process them privately.

− Children need to be shown affection and encouraged to learn about their emotions.

Like to say 'yes' – *It's fine if you want to play your music.*

Do you enjoy saying 'yes' to your children without feeling that your authority is threatened?

+ The more you allow your children to explore and express themselves (safely), the better.
− There will be times when you must say 'no'.

Prefer to say 'no' – *Turn that music off!*

Do you find yourself saying 'no' more often than you say 'yes' and feeling that it is important for your authority to do so?

+ It is essential that children have clear boundaries.
− If you always say 'no', your children will stop asking your permission and simply do it anyway.

Praise – *I'm sure you'll do well.*

Do you like to find positive ways of motivating your child, always assuming that he can do anything?

+ Being positive with your child is very important and will help to give him confidence.

– If you only ever praise your child, he will never work out when you are less pleased with him.

Blame – *That's typical of you to spoil it.*

Do you find yourself criticizing your child more often than praising her?

+ Children need to know when they have done wrong.

– Unless you also praise your child, ideally at least three times as much as you blame her, she is unlikely to develop confidently.

Coaching – *Let's work this out together.*

Do you like to listen to your child and work out the best ways of doing things together?

+   Providing practical suggestions that suit your child is a really good way of helping him learn.

–   Occasionally, it can be quicker just to say what you would do rather than work it out together.

Telling – *Do it this way.*

Are you normally sure that there is only one way of doing things? Do you find it easier to tell your child what to do rather than work it out together?

±   Sometimes explaining simple things to your child works well. Children learn by doing, so it is important to give them opportunities to do this.

Adults always know best – *There's only one way of doing this.*

Do you like to think that you will always know better than your child?

+ There are many situations when adults do know best.

− There are many situations when children are much more likely to know best.

Adults sometimes know best – *Let's try your way – it might be better.*

Do you sometimes think that your child is much more likely to have a better way of doing something than you do?

+ Allowing your child to take the lead and create solutions is helping her to grow as a learner.

− In some situations there is an adult responsibility that it would be silly of you to avoid.

Comfortable with conflict – *Let's sort this out together.*

Are you comfortable even when your child disagrees with you and happy to work out the best solution together?

+ Working your way through conflict is an essential life skill that you are helping your child to learn.

— Too much conflict is unhelpful and not good for learning.

Avoid conflict – *Let's hope this sorts itself out.*

Do you prefer to hide away when your children are angry or emotional and hope that things will sort themselves out?

+ Not jumping in as the parent to sort things out allows children to learn how to work things through on their own.

— It is very easy for conflict to fester and for children to become aggressive if adults do not help them to work things through.

Did you find it easy to work out the ways you tend to behave as a parent? It will largely depend on the situation as to which choice in each case is most helpful. For example, if your child is young and not yet confident about walking, you will need to stay close. But if your child is managing to work out how to climb on to something and is not in danger, you might prefer to hang back and let him or her work it out.

Five principles of happy parenting

As mentioned on page 101, there is no right or wrong parenting style. Different situations require different styles. However, if you parent in the same way all the time, it may be that you are missing a trick. You might like to come back to the 'choices' illustrated next time you feel that things did not go quite as you had hoped, and have a think about other styles you could adopt. Some of the choices relating to your parenting style are more fundamental than those explored earlier because they affect almost all the roles you play. These are examined next.

Principle 1: Be positive

This is the second specific mention in *Happy Families* of the importance of a positive mindset, and in every chapter it has existed as an underlying principle, so it must be important. But in this chapter it is especially so.

Your attitude to life affects not just you and your partner – it also fundamentally influences your children's chance of happiness. Our primary task as parents is to see beyond the immediate and keep faith with our children. We have to hold on to our belief in their potential and value as human beings, even when their behaviour seems deliberately designed to disprove such idealistic notions. We have to give our children what is sometimes referred to as 'unconditional love'. This is the golden seed that we can 'plant' in them to help them to grow up happily.

How did you view pages 102–13? Did you see yourself as more of an optimist than a pessimist? (You saw in Chapter 1 how you can learn to be more optimistic.) Do you tend to say 'yes' or 'no' to your children? Clearly, both are required. ('Can we watch the TV for another five hours?' 'Can we make pizza with you today?') And what about the number of times you praise your children? Do you tend to praise more than you blame?

While it seems that some adults are temperamentally more optimistic than others (although this can change), all children need a positive environment in which to grow up, and this is something that parents can strongly influence.

Where is parenting learnt?

▶ Think back to your own childhood for a moment. What do you remember about the way your parents treated you? Did they say things such as, 'I am so pleased about the way you did that' and 'Thanks very much for helping'? Or were their comments more of the 'You're useless' and 'You're always so messy' variety?

▶ Can you remember how hurt and bad you felt when you received the second kind of comments as a child?

There are two very good reasons for parenting your children positively: it will help them to feel good about themselves, and it will also help them to be more successful in every sense of the word.

We all need to feel good about ourselves

In the next chapter we will explore esteem in more detail, but at this point I just want to appeal to your common sense. Imagine that someone you know is trying to get you to do something for them with these words:

> 'Although you are really lazy, do you think you could surprise us all by doing something useful for a change? I want you to go to the supermarket and buy the ingredients for our picnic.'

How would this make you feel? Would you be likely to respond favourably? What if the request were put this way?

> 'You're so good at choosing interesting ingredients, Bill. Could you possibly go to the supermarket and choose a picnic for us?'

The second of these approaches works well because it makes you feel good about yourself. Words like this are what parents need to surround their children with so that they feel good and want to do things.

Accentuate the positive

How many ways can you come up with to praise your child and make him feel good about himself? Overleaf are a few comments to get you going.

Well done! Thanks. Great work! I am so pleased... I've really been looking forward to seeing you. You're so good at... That's really impressive. That must have taken a lot of effort.

If these kinds of remark do not come naturally to you, practise saying them, perhaps alone at first. When you say them for real, you must sound as though you mean them because children are very quick to spot a fake.

Surrounding your child with a positive take on the world will really help him. It does not stop you pointing out things that he could do better or differently. But it provides a really strong basis from which to teach him things.

The power of words

The second reason you need to be positive involves a simple piece of psychology, sometimes referred to as the 'self-fulfilling prophecy'. Put simply, if you tell someone they are good at something, they are more likely to succeed at it. If you tell someone they are hopeless, they are likely to become hopeless. If you prophesy that your child can do something ('You're doing really well; I'm sure you can finish off your cereal now'), she probably will. If you prophesy that she will not be able to do something ('You stupid child; that's far too difficult for you!'), she will almost certainly fail.

The effect of your words is really powerful. You can literally shape your children's likely happiness by consciously training yourself to look for the positive and then commenting on it.

As you get really confident at this, you can deliberately try to catch them at the actual moment they are being successful and praise them right then. The more specific you can be, the better; they will then understand what they are being praised for: 'I really liked the way you cleared up your room without me having to remind me. Well done!'

Sometimes you may have to help them when they come up with negative language:

> **Child:** I can't do this homework, Dad, it's too hard.
> **Dad:** Would you like me to have a look at it with you?
> **Child:** Maybe...
> **Dad:** You've already made a good start. Let's have another go. I think you can do this – the numbers are just a bit bigger than the sums you did earlier. Do you want me to help you now?
> **Child:** No, it's all right, Dad. I can do it myself...

By constantly helping your child to change 'can't' to 'can' you are making a very practical and positive contribution to his well-being.

After a few exchanges like this your child will also begin to see you as a really useful resource. Of course, he will not always be able to do things and you will have tears and tantrums along the way. But gradually he will learn the kind of persistence that will stand him in good stead throughout his life.

And the next time you come to be talking about something your child has done in the past but is apprehensive about doing again, you can go one stage further. You can simply assume that he will find ways of achieving what he wants to do and actively help him to prepare for it with success in mind.

Actions speak louder than words

Words work, but what you actually do is even more important. Mahatma Gandhi used to talk about 'being the change you want to become', by which I think he meant that if you want people to do things, you need to show them the way. This is especially true for parents and their children, for you are the most powerful role models in their life. They will imitate you, not just your mannerisms and patterns of speech, but the way you do things and the values you appear to uphold.

Children who wave their hands around in distress at the first sighting of a wasp in summer may well have a mother or father who does the same. Those who give up easily and start crying may be the children of parents who give up easily and start shouting when they are stuck.

Children will be influenced by you whether you are acting positively or negatively. So as an adult, you need to decide what behaviour you want your children to have and then model it. If you want them to say 'please' and 'thank you', no amount of telling will work if you do not use these words yourself. Equally, if you want them to sit at the table and eat in a civilized manner while you are constantly wandering around with a snack in your hand, they may see one rule operating for you and one for them (and prefer your version).

How to stay positive

Sometimes it can be helpful to have tactics that enable you to stay positive with your children when things are not going so well. Here are three to get you started.

Distraction: If your child is unhappy or grumpy, produce a rival attraction to help take her mind off whatever is bothering her.

Laughter: If necessary, pull a silly face or make a fool of yourself. It's worth the embarrassment of it, although once your children reach their teens, this particular tactic can be counter-productive.

Imagination: Imagine you are on another planet. Don't get drawn into your child's world all the time. Stay on planet Cheerful and talk calmly to him about how you can help him fix whatever is causing him unhappiness.

Principle 2: Be consistent

When actor Bill Cosby once said, 'Even though your kids will consistently do the exact opposite of what you're telling them to do, you have to keep loving them just as much,' he was alluding to both the perversity of human nature (we love to do what we are told not to do) and the consistency of cause and effect in parenting.

This section explores what it means to be consistent and why it needs to be a core part of any parent's life.

Of course, if you want to be consistent, you have to work out what you are consistent to. As there are no prizes for being consistently inconsistent, it will pay you to think through what matters to you with your partner or, if you are a lone parent, with a trusted friend or family member. You might like to do this once you have read the next few pages and have a clearer idea about the areas you want to explore. Essentially, we are going to be looking at rules and routines. When do you say 'no'? What do you do when your child disobeys you? How do you create patterns of expected activity during your day that make everyone's life easier?

The importance of rules

For some reason many people associate rules with oppression, rigidity and a lack of creativity. But, in fact, if you choose the right ones, they will help you relax and live happily together. If you want to see a good example of how not to do this, by the way, look no further than Roald Dahl's *Charlie and the Chocolate Factory* (1967). This shows that when children are given no boundaries, mayhem follows. Veruca learns that if she yells enough, she can always get her way. Mike Teavee addles his brain by endlessly watching television. Augustus gets fat on his unrestricted diet, and Violet's gum chewing, like her addiction to trophies, is totally obsessive. Each of these children's parents forgot one of the basic principles of parenting – that children need clear and consistent boundaries.

At the most fundamental level, rules are your way of sharing with your children what you believe in and of transmitting your values to them. Rules are the glue that ensures you all stick to your beliefs (or at least as close to them as possible). If, for example, you are committed to a particular faith, you may have very strong pacifist views that may lead you to have certain rules in your house, such as no gun play. If you believe very strongly in the importance of democracy, involving your children in democratic processes early on in their life may matter to you. Or if civilized mealtimes are a priority, you may have rules about passing things to each other, not starting before everyone has their food, not getting down before each person has finished, helping to clear away, and so on.

At another fundamental level, rules are a way of ensuring that a group of people functions effectively. That's why even very 'primitive' tribes have rules and customs that they observe, such as someone staying awake at night to ensure the survival of the group, and standard ways of greeting strangers to be sure about their intentions. Shared rules help you to have a feeling of belonging: you are part of a team with a similar game plan. It is a short step from observing rules to feeling solidarity, and you can hear this when a member of your family says, 'We think that...', 'We always...', 'In our family we...'

These are by and large helpful statements for your children to make. It shows that they have understood a rule and taken responsibility for putting it into practice. Obviously, it should not be taken so far as to become inflexible. And children need to learn that different households have different rules (just as schools do).

When you talk about rules at home you are really discussing behaviour: what is acceptable and what is not. Rules are a kind of shorthand that you can use to avoid having to explain the impact of certain kinds of behaviour each time they occur. (For example, starting your food before others have theirs gives out a message of selfishness and turns the meal into a kind of competition to see who can finish first.)

Generally speaking, there are three things to think about when working out the rules of your house:

- What is reasonable?
- What is appropriate for the age of the child?
- Is it necessary?

Reasonable rules

As the name suggests, a reasonable rule is something that seems reasonable to you and your family. Generally, you need rules only for things that are or might be problems. So having a rule for what to do in the event of being attacked by a lion may be reasonable in some parts of Africa, but is clearly ridiculous in suburban Britain. On the other hand, helping your child to see that he should not talk to strangers and never accept a lift from a stranger may, sadly, be an essential part of survival everywhere.

How you express rules may vary. 'Never put your finger into an electric socket' and 'Don't get down from the table until everyone has finished eating' are prohibitions that begin with a negative word. But using 'always' at the beginning of a rule ('Always wash your hands before meals') turns it into a positive statement rather than a negative prohibition. The more you can maintain this positive approach, the better, as you have already discovered.

Rules suited to age

Of course, it makes sense to have rules that take the age of your child into account. While being respectful of others and never hitting people are likely to be eternal rules, not going out of your sight is clearly aimed at toddlers, while using a mobile phone to call home is more relevant to teenagers.

Rules will change as children grow up and your family circumstances change. What makes sense in one house – 'Always stay well back from the fireplace' – may seem unnecessary in a house that has only radiators, for example.

Let children decide as much as possible

If you want your children to turn into responsible adults, having too many rules is not a good idea because they need to learn how to take decisions for themselves.

Another good reason for not having too many rules is that you will have to enforce them, and this can make any parent's life a misery.

Perhaps as you read this you are realizing that you have not really agreed any rules in your house. If so, now might be the moment to see if you can. Or maybe you are wondering how you might start introducing new rules in the light of what you have recently been thinking about. If either of these descriptions fits you, try some of these suggestions:

▶ Make sure that you and your partner, or any other important carer in your child's life, are in agreement about rules.

▶ Plan well in advance, especially if the rule is not likely to go down well with your children.

▶ Take it gently. Don't try to change too many areas at one time.

▶ Go through new rules carefully with your children, talking them through what they will mean in practice.

▶ Reinforce rules by referring to them constantly when they are not about to be used so that your child really does understand them.

▶ Work out what really matters to you and stick to that, while being prepared to be more flexible about less important areas.

▶ Be open. Explain when something is not working, and involve your children in deciding on how you can do it differently.

▶ Keep a diary or record of what happens so that you can note the progress (and challenges) along the way.

▶ Reward your children for doing what you ask them to.

▶ Reward yourself and anyone else involved when things begin to improve as a result of rules you have introduced.

Routines matter too

Just as rules are the wheels of family life, so routines are the oil that keeps them turning. Free spirits sometimes frown on routines, but don't take any notice. You need them for your sanity.

Getting up, leaving the house in the morning, eating meals, getting ready for bed, reading together, going to sleep...so many things just work better if you have a basic routine for them. Once the routine is really established, you can vary it, but if you want to be happy as a parent, invest time and effort in establishing clear-cut ways of doing things, and encourage preferred patterns of behaviour and habits.

The way to establish a routine is, of course, to practise it. But before you do so, it is worth spending time thinking through the sequence of steps you will need. If this sounds pedantic, just pause to consider what you would do with a puppy. You would work out how you want it to behave – not peeing indoors, sitting when asked, not jumping up, coming when called – then train it to do these things. The training itself would require constant repetition and praise until the dog gets the message.

In many ways, training a child is not dissimilar, but many people invest more time and energy in working out how to train their puppy than they do in establishing routines for their children.

How good are your routines?

Look at the chart overleaf and take a moment to consider some areas where routines can be helpful. Add in any others that are not covered here, then give yourself a rating in the last three columns for your own performance.

Routine	Working well	Could be improved	Need to establish
Getting up			
Going to sleep			
Getting out of the house in the morning			
Getting ready for bed			
Mealtimes			
Reading together			
Putting toys away			
Saying thank you			

A few hours spent in establishing routines, even enduring a few tears along the way, will repay the time you invest ten times over. For routines are close cousins of habits: they are the things you do on auto-pilot without having to stop and think. And because you do them automatically, so much time that would otherwise be spent arguing is saved. Life as a parent consequently becomes less challenging.

Ideally, if there are two of you doing the parenting, you will get your act together and both establish identical routines. However, children are so flexible that they will easily survive different ways of doing things. So in some homes there is Dad's way, Mum's way, a step-parent's or a grandparent's way of doing things. Children readily accept this, which is just as well because when they go off to school, they will suddenly begin to discover that routines + personality = different ways of doing things.

Principle 3: Coach more than you tell

In the bad old days children knew their place because adults told them where it was. They also told them what to do and how to do it. For some aspects of life this approach works well. 'Don't touch that' (if something is dangerous), and 'Sit down, please, we are still eating' are perfectly reasonable and effective ways of dealing with common occurrences.

But for most situations that you are likely to encounter there are two good reasons why telling needs to be used sparingly. First, it is dehumanizing, and second, it does not work as well as coaching.

Do you tell or coach?

▷ Look back to page 111 for a moment. Did you find that you tend to coach your child more than tell?

▷ In which situations do you tend to coach?

▷ Do you feel confident in what it is to be a coach?

Treat children like people

Do you ever feel that what you say is largely ignored by your offspring? Do you sometimes feel that you are ineffective as a parent? Having fixed preconceptions of what parenting should entail can make you feel inadequate, but it's important not to become obsessed about your role. Your relationship with your children is unbalanced because they are dependent upon you. Whether it feels like it or not, you have a lot of power. Without parents, children have no access to food, shelter, affection or any other basic building blocks of life.

In our culture parents tend to assume an excessive degree of responsibility for their children's development, and forget that at one level the parent/child situation is simply a relationship between two human beings. As such, many of the principles that work in other relationships also apply here.

A good rule of thumb when dealing with a child is to think about how you would respond if someone treated you in a similar fashion. Do you like it when someone gives you lots of orders? Would you continue to be friends with someone who patronizes you or criticizes everything you do?

If you get into the habit of telling your children to do things all the time, this is likely to degenerate into nagging, and from there into shouting at each other. This is undignified for a parent, and ineffective as a means of getting your children to do the things you want. It also does little to encourage a sense of responsibility in your child. Coaching, on the other hand, gets things done with your child taking full responsibility.

Coaching works

The idea of coaching sports has long been familiar, but now the term is applied to a much broader range of activities. Coaching involves one person (normally a parent, although siblings can coach each other) helping a child to achieve something for herself. This may require helping her to see exactly what is going on at present, where she wants to get to and how best she might do this.

You can coach a child to:

- Learn a new skill
- Improve self-esteem
- Learn how to deal with emotions
- Change behaviour

Coaching involves patience, understanding, self-control and good communication skills – all qualities that parents should already have or be on the way to acquiring.

Let's imagine that you want to help a child learn to ride a bike. You can either tell her what to do: 'Get on the bike and just start riding', or you could adopt a coaching approach: 'Yesterday you did really well. How about trying to ride with me walking alongside, ready to catch you if you start to fall over?'

The way you talk to your child can have a huge impact on her confidence and self-esteem. Study the RESPECT model below (developed by Alistair Smith and me) to see the kinds of thing you might want to say to your child when you are in coaching mode.

The RESPECT method

- Concentrates on what your child is doing
- Gives positive feedback
- Motivates your child to want to get better

To achieve these things parents should try to be:

Reassuring
Learning new things is hard, so finding ways of reassuring your child will show her that you understand this. 'I know this may seem difficult at first, so just take it gently.'

Enthusiastic
Positive feedback helps learners. 'I really like the way you kept going, even though it was difficult for you.'

Steady
Children need patient and consistent support. 'Take your time. I am happy to help you for as long as you'd like me to.'

Practical
Giving your child practical advice about how he can improve is a really good way of helping. 'You might like to try putting your foot here to stop you falling off.'

Engaging
It helps if you can motivate your child. 'If you keep on improving like this, you are really going to see the difference.'

Clear
Giving your child specific tips helps too. 'If you use both hands, you might find it easier.'

Truthful
It will not help your child if you exaggerate too much or if you hide the truth from her. 'You're not as good at writing as you are at reading at the moment, so let's practise shaping your letters, shall we?'

How to be a parent/coach

When you or your child identify something that has to be learnt – using a knife and fork, for example, or riding a bike – you need to watch and listen as your child tries to do it, and perhaps set aside time to give further help. On other occasions, you might just need to boost confidence ('I'm no good at anything, Mum'), or change behaviour (perhaps when your child needs to learn persistence and not give up on difficult tasks), or deal with emotions (perhaps when your child is having tantrums). In this last case you need to wait until it occurs, unless there are things you can do beforehand to prevent it.

As you observe, you should give feedback to your child on what you see, and make encouraging remarks to help him to persevere, using the RESPECT framework to guide you.

Often you need to ask questions rather than make comments. 'How does that feel?' 'When you hold it like this, is it more comfortable?' 'How many times would you like to practise this?'

You need to take great care to focus on what your child is doing and not on her personality. So, for example, focus on the fact that your child is hitting another person and ask her to stop doing it, rather than telling her that she is a nasty, violent person. Timing matters, too. If your child has become distressed, you might be better off helping her to calm down before you offer any advice or feedback.

With your coaching help, your child will get better. And all the while she will be learning how to do it on her own so that she is not dependent on you. Once she begins to make improvements, your role as a coach is to praise her and motivate her to see it through.

Incidentally, a coaching mentality is useful not just for parenting, but also to help any member of your family (or a work colleague) to do something that they cannot do currently. The great thing about coaching is that you do not have to be an expert in the subject to be able to help someone else. If you want to test this out, have some family fun by trying this simple coaching activity.

Can you coach?

▷ Get hold of a bucket and a tennis ball. Give the ball to the person who is going to be coached and put the bucket three paces behind him. His goal is to get the ball into the bucket by throwing it over his shoulder. As the coach, you can watch, question and give feedback to help the person learning how to do it. Notice the improvement, even if you are not at all good at ball-throwing yourself.

Setting goals

In order to be an effective parent/coach you will need to plan ahead and help your child to set some short-term goals. A goal is something you want to do by a certain time or date. By setting goals you can make things happen rather than let them happen by chance.

How you talk about goals with your child matters. Take a moment to look at these three examples:

▷ I want you to get better at music.
▷ I want you to get better at playing the piano.
▷ By the end of term I want you to be able to play this piano piece without looking at the music.

Which comment is the most useful? Of course, it's the last one because it sets a specific goal, has a realistic target date and can be measured. In other words, you can easily see if you've succeeded or failed. However, the child must want to learn his piano piece as much as his parent wants him to if this strategy is to be really effective.

Take a moment to think about all those things that you would like your child to learn in the next few years. Are there any that might lend themselves particularly well to goal-setting?

What would you like to coach?

Using this chart, make a note of a few things on which you would like to act as a parent/coach with your child.

Coaching goals	My plans		
	By next week	*By next month*	*By end of year*

Always focus on one issue at a time and make real progress with it before tackling others.

As an American football coach called George Foreman once put it: 'Everybody wants to be somebody. The thing you have to do is give them confidence they can. You have to give a kid a dream.'

Principle 4: Get organized

It's five o'clock. You are in the garden. At about this time every day your children get hungry. You have some food in the fridge and in the cupboard, but you can't remember what. Your children seem to be happy enough playing together. Time drifts on.

Cut to a scene in the kitchen just thirty minutes later. Your children are fractious. You are hassled. No one seems to want the food you are serving up. And then your partner walks in through the door…

The vast majority of things that go wrong for parents result from a lack of organization. Boring but true.

Getting the food on the table before everyone's blood sugar level becomes dangerously low is just one small example of this. I am sure you can think of many others.

In fact, getting organized is a much more fundamental part of being an effective and happy parent because it begs a question: organized for what? There are many different answers to this, and here are just a few.

- To make mealtimes happier.
- To spend more time with my children.
- To spend more time with a partner or close friend.
- To spend time doing the things that matter.
- To make me feel more confident.
- To keep my stress levels down.
- To be able to balance my work life and my home life.
- To be able to work longer hours.
- To be able to work fewer hours.

You, and only you, know how to achieve these things. There is rarely a right or wrong way, and how you get organized may depend on your state of life or state of mind. But one thing is pretty certain. Unless you actually want to spend time with your nearest and dearest, being a happy family will have to remain a dream.

Many parents I meet use the phrase 'quality time' to describe the kind of time they want to spend with their children. I happen to dislike this phrase, and I suspect that many parents are deluding themselves when they use it. What they really mean is that in order to fit their children into their busy lives, they expect their children to be ready and available whenever they are. This rarely works. Children take time to relax, and rarely do well when they feel they are 'on parade'. (Think how your own stress levels about a special family event have mysteriously transmitted themselves to your children and they choose that moment to play up.)

Quality time can be a tacit admission of a life with too much packed into it. Children need lots of time – and a regular time. ('Monday's the day I go swimming with Dad.' 'On Fridays Granny picks me up from school.')

Finding time is a real issue, especially for families who are not all living together under the same roof. Stepfathers can find this very challenging, especially if they work unpredictable hours. Setting aside a regular afternoon after school is one way of making sure you have consistent time together. While it has a different quality from weekend time, it is no less valuable. Indeed, from a child's perspective, going away for a weekend to see father or mother in a different home and possibly with a different partner can itself bring pressures, so time spent one-to-one during the week can actually be more relaxed.

Working backwards from the desired result

At the heart of good organization are a clock, a plan and a mindset. Assuming you want to do something (that's the mindset part), you need to be clear in your own head exactly when the task needs to be finished.

Think about the suppertime example on page 127. The desired result might have been to have tea on the table by five o'clock. The organization bit begins earlier that day, when you check whether you have all the ingredients for, say, scrambled eggs and peas. How long does it take you to lay the table, whisk the eggs and cook them? Five minutes? Ten minutes? Twenty minutes? What about if you have interruptions, such as another child arriving home, or a younger child hanging on to your coat tails? It is always worth adding an extra ten minutes or so to allow for those inevitable distractions that are part of family life.

While this may seem patronizingly obvious, the point is to show that there is no way around these organizational building blocks if you want to be on top of your parenting. No matter how simple or complicated the scenario, you need to be able to organize yourself, and you also need to help your children become good at organizing themselves.

Being organized is as much a state of mind as it is a specific set of skills – less about scrambling eggs than about what has to happen for supper to be ready on time in order to keep everyone cheerful. Parenting does not come with a crystal ball. The unexpected is bound to happen, but in the meantime, you might as well plan for the expected, such as children getting bored on long journeys and forgetting things they need for school.

Get more organized

Here are some approaches that might help you to improve your organizational ability.

One-to-ones
Set up a regular time to do things with different members of your family. This might be daily, or happen as infrequently as once a month. Remember, it's much better to promise and deliver than to cancel too often.

Plan ahead
Create a family diary. Put everyone's key commitments in it. If you have a school-age child, make sure that you and the child are aware of homework commitments.

Weekly meetings
Have a regular time when you share information, and give each member of the family a chance to check that they have understood.

Chore charts

Share out the household tasks, making sure that everyone has some, that they are regularly checked and that each person is thanked for completing them. You could do this on one big list displayed prominently in the kitchen and/or make individual charts for each person.

Checklists

It's essential to keep a list of things that you always need to do or remember, such as tasks to be completed before leaving the house in the morning, or before you go to bed, or before you can watch TV. Keep the really important things at the top of the list and do these first.

Games box

Teach your children games that they can play without you, and build up a box of games that do not depend on your involvement. Having another set of games that work well on journeys is also a good idea.

Wet weather box

Have a box containing dressing-up clothes, puzzle books, comics and games for those days when it is hard to get outside.

Tidy bedrooms

Making sure your children can get to their bed without tripping over days of discarded toys and clothes will help them to stay organized, as will ensuring that they have adequate storage space for their things.

Paperwork

In a busy home important envelopes get opened in many different rooms. Try to have one central place where you put bills, reminders and letters from your child's school. (It is essential to extract school correspondence from your child every evening as a matter of routine, or you will miss out on crucial information and the child will miss out on school trips.)

Being organized may seem very mundane in comparison with all the exciting things you could be doing, but experience shows that it can be the gateway to real happiness as a parent.

Principle 5: Be strong, but admit mistakes

When you read the word 'strong' what comes into your mind? Physical strength? Power? Always being right? Have you ever watched a parent in action and thought to yourself, 'Don't be so weak! Insist she stops doing that straight away,' and then gone home and almost immediately found yourself in a similar situation?

Being a parent calls for enormous strength of will and physical stamina. But the kind of strength it requires is different from the strength you might need to get on in the workplace.

Look back at the parent roles described on pages 102–13. Which of the alternatives suggested seem the stronger positions to adopt? Does it depend on the situation, or are some ways of doing things inherently weaker than others? And what about personality? Do some parents show their strength in different ways?

What is a strong parent?

Being strong as a parent involves many things, some of which are listed below.

- Consistently showing your love for your family
- Enforcing the rules you have created
- Saying 'no' and meaning it
- Saying 'yes' and meaning it
- Staying calm
- Presenting a united front whenever you parent with another adult
- Asking for advice
- Admitting mistakes and saying sorry
- Being selfish (sometimes)

Countless research studies from throughout the world show that strong parents tend to be happier and to raise happier children.

Show your love

As you have seen throughout *Happy Families* so far, showing unconditional love to your children is one of the greatest gifts you can bestow on them. But how do you do it when you are boiling inside because they just will not do what you say? Or when, after a long day's work and with an early start the next morning, they keep you up for half the night apparently for no good reason? Here are some approaches that I find helpful.

- Tell your child that you love him. If you find this difficult to fit in during the day, come up with some reassuring words that you can use every night before he goes to sleep: for example, 'Night night. Love you lots. See you in the morning.'
- Make sure, whatever has gone before, that you always end the day on a positive note.
- Keep using positive words with your child, even if that is not how you are feeling.
- Praise your child in front of other people (unless you know that this causes her embarrassment).
- When your child is upset or angry, show him your affection physically, with a hug or other sign, whatever he likes.

Present a united front

Have you ever watched a couple out for lunch openly disagreeing about what their misbehaving children should and should not do at the table? It's painful. There are few things more designed to undermine a parent than presenting a divided front to children. If you have a partner, it is really important for you to agree what matters to you both and then stick to it. Sometimes one of you may have to compromise your personal point of view so that you can at least agree in front of your offspring.

Children have a unique ability to spot differences and mercilessly exploit them. You don't want to be in a family where children appeal to each parent or carer separately because they are likely to get a different answer.

Being united can be especially difficult when your children spend time in more than one home as a consequence of divorce or separation. Ideally, parents in these situations will agree common approaches to major issues, but often this is simply not possible. Indeed, when parents split up, it is often because they have fundamentally different views of the world, so they are unlikely to agree on common positions after the split if they were unable to do so before.

If you are in this situation, the more you can avoid any comparisons between your way of doing things and your ex's, the better. It will only invite your child to see this as a source of possible weakness and to exploit the fact that you set different boundaries.

Enforce your rules

On pages 118 and 121 you read about the importance of setting clear boundaries and establishing routines. In a sense, that's the easy bit.

It's enforcing your rules when they are *not* accepted that is most challenging.

The first thing to be clear about with your partner (if appropriate) is those things that really matter to you. For example, you may think it important to ensure that your child does not watch a film containing sexual or violent material, whereas it is undesirable (but not so serious) if she goes to school with dirty shoes.

Once you have found your baseline issues, you need to stick to your views. If your child disobeys you, it is essential to follow things through, keeping to your point and, if necessary, punishing your child if you want to have a happy life. This may cause short-term pain, but will almost always bring long-term gain.

An important technique in this respect involves helping your child to see two things: first, that he can choose what he does, and second, that there are consequences to his actions.

Take the issue that many parents find tough: ensuring that a child watches only films that are appropriate for his age. The pressure on you may well be intense – 'Everybody else is allowed to'; 'Don't be so mean, Dad'. And there will come a time when, having explained your reasons (you love him too much to allow him to be damaged by stuff, and anyway it's what the law says; that's why film classifications were introduced), you will simply not be prepared to endure another argument on the subject.

At this point you may want to make it clear that if your child continues to challenge you about the kind of films he is allowed to watch, you will stop him watching any television at all for a specified number of days.

If you are indeed challenged, you must carry out your threat to stop all TV as you have indicated. You may have to endure anger and stroppiness, but it will be worth it.

Say 'no' and mean it

Here and overleaf are three ways of dealing with a child who wants more than you are prepared to give.

> **Child:** Can I watch *The Bill*, please?
> **Parent:** No.
> **Child:** Oh, please…
> **Parent:** Not now.
> **Child:** Toby's allowed to, so why can't I?
> **Parent:** Because you can't.
> **Child:** Just ten minutes of it.
> **Parent:** Just ten, and I mean it.

(Parent goes off to clear up the kitchen and returns 15 minutes later.)
Parent: Time to turn it off now.
(Child appears not to hear.)
Parent: I said, time to turn it off now.
Child: I'll turn it off when we get to the adverts.
Parent: OK.

Recognize this sort of scenario? It's one of those all-too-common conversations where a parent says 'no', but so weakly that the child is learning that it can be turned into a 'yes'. What would you have done differently? Here's how it might have gone.

Child: Can I watch *The Bill*, please?
Parent: No.
Child: Oh, please…
Parent: Not now. If you really want to watch it, you can record it and watch it tomorrow.
Child: OK, then.

This second exchange doesn't immediately nip the problem in the bud, but you can still catch it later, as the third exchange shows:

Child: Can I watch *The Bill*, please?
Parent: No.
Child: Oh, please…
Parent: Not now.
Child: Toby's allowed to, so why can't I?
Parent: On this occasion I am prepared to let you watch just ten minutes, but I need to know that the moment I ask you to turn it off, you will do so. Is that clear?
Child: Yes, Mum.
(Nine minutes later parent returns.)
Parent: Just one more minute.
(One minute goes by.)
Parent: Off now, please.
Child: OK.
(Child turns TV off.)
Parent: Well done.

Holding firm is tough when children are capable of wheedling, making unflattering comparisons, tears, anger, tantrums and so on. Their tactics amount to a form of torture. But every time you say 'no' and end up giving in, you are making it much harder for yourself next time round.

Say 'yes' and mean it

Some people find saying 'yes' and meaning it similarly hard. This can happen when your child asks permission to do something and you say 'yes' because:

- You can't face another argument.
- You were not really listening and it sounded a harmless enough request.
- You hope that if you say yes and do nothing, your child will forget.
- You hadn't realized that the child cannot do it alone, but will need your help or active involvement.

These are just four of the commoner reasons, but there are many more.

If you say 'yes' and don't deliver, you run the risk of undermining yourself in a different way (see page 117 to remind yourself how actions speak louder than words). It's an inescapable truth that every time you fail to deliver on a clear commitment, you run the risk of undermining the trust that your child has for you.

Knowing this, you might like to build in a moment's thinking time before you say 'yes' without really being sure what you are agreeing to. Develop responses such as, 'So are you asking me if you can...', which will give you time to work out whether the request is a reasonable one.

Stay calm

All parents lose their cool sometimes because we are all human. But the more you can keep calm deep inside (where it matters), the better. If you can manage your emotions effectively, you will exude a confidence and certainty that you might not feel.

Sometimes it may be necessary to ignore certain kinds of poor behaviour in order to stay detached and not get drawn into something that the child can work out for himself. If, for example, he is engaged in a temporary screaming fit because you have told him not to do something, the chances are that after ten minutes of his getting no reaction from you, normality will return. This kind of approach is easier to manage within the confines of your own home than on, say, a trip to the supermarket, where it would be very difficult to hold your nerve. You need to use this tactic sparingly and accompany it with lots of praise when things go well, or your child will begin to think that you do not care, rather than thinking that you choose not to take any notice when he is making a scene.

Ask for advice

Read the problem pages of magazines and newspapers and you will see countless letters asking for advice about intimate matters of love and sex. Yet, by comparison, there are very few about parenting issues. Maybe this is because there is still such a stigma attached to being a struggling parent. It is even possible to find yourself in prison for not making sure your child goes to school, or to receive an ASBO (anti-social behaviour order) on account of things that your child does.

If you're having difficulties, the most obvious and sensible thing to do is to ask for advice. At its simplest level it has been found that parents who have a good network of friends and family tend to feel more confident about their parenting. So get together with other parents, formally or informally. Get into the habit of sharing problems and their solutions. Read as widely as you can, adapting and modifying ideas (like those in *Happy Families*) to suit your own situation. See also Further Reading and Useful Addresses, pages 211–14.

Admit mistakes

In times gone by parents were always right. In fact, most authority figures – teachers, doctors, lawyers, politicians – were always right. Of course, this cannot always be the case.

In today's complex world, admitting a mistake is especially important. And sometimes you might need to apologize directly to your child for making a hasty or incorrect judgement. Contrary to much received wisdom, this is a sign of strength, not of weakness. Provided the apology or admission of fault is genuine, it is likely to strengthen your relationship with the person concerned.

Naturally, there are limits to the number of times it is smart to make errors, especially the same ones. As Oscar Wilde (1854–1900) remarked, 'Experience is simply the name we give our mistakes.'

Be selfish

Strange as it may seem, you need to be selfish as a parent from time to time. Management guru Charles Handy has an expression for this: he calls it 'proper selfishness'. This kind of selfishness is essential to the maintenance and growth of you as an individual. Without it you will become so mentally and physically run down that you are unlikely to be an effective or happy parent.

Assuming there are no safety issues involved, indulging in some proper selfishness can mean:

▶ Asking your child to amuse himself
▶ Taking time off and getting your partner or a friend to look after your child
▶ Having a night out without children
▶ Having proper adult time with your partner or a close friend

Parenting expert Steve Biddulph has come up with an interesting idea. In couples where one person goes out to work and the other works at home looking after the children, he suggests that at homecoming time the first thing you should do is banish the children and take ten minutes together as a couple to drink, eat and catch up with each other.

I propose a modification to this because it seems unnecessarily harsh on children who may well have been looking forward to seeing their mum or dad. Why not spend the first ten minutes or so as a family, bonding and chatting, and then, provided your children are not hungry or tired, the adults can grab some time together to be properly selfish.

Whether you adopt either of these suggestions or not, the principle of looking after yourself is an important one, and you can read more about it in Chapter 8.

Troubleshooting

This chapter has covered a wide range of issues, and space permits me to address only a few of the recurring worries about them in this section. However, I hope my suggestions will start some trains of thought in you that prove helpful.

It's lonely being a single parent.

Yes, it can be. And that sense of loneliness can be even stronger if you feel you are carrying sole responsibility for the children. If feasible, make sure that your ex-partner continues to play an active role in the parenting of your children and that you are not left making all the major decisions. If the situation allows, and it is judged to be in the interests of your children, encourage your ex-partner to play an active and regular role in childcare, not least because this will give you much-needed opportunities to get out, meet friends and recharge your batteries.

There are some good single-parent networks out there that can be a source of helpful advice and make you feel more supported (see page 214). Also, however tempting it may become, try not to withdraw socially: make sure that you are taking your children to groups and activities where you can meet other parents and potentially make new friends yourself.

I don't like the way my stepchildren behave.

While the biological parent ultimately carries responsibility for matters of discipline, that is not to say that much of the power and responsibility cannot be shared with you. The key is to have some careful and thorough negotiations with the biological parent about the extent to which they are happy to let you parent, and the degree to which they will support you in the disciplining and nurturing of their children.

If children are behaving badly in your presence, they may well be feeling hostile and are likely to use any opportunity to create friction between you and your partner. Do your best to support the biological parent when they discipline the children, and don't try to court popularity by undermining what they say or do.

Although you may not have much scope to impose additional consequences for bad behaviour, you can always set your own boundary by telling your partner and/or the children how you feel about the children's behaviour towards you and withdrawing promptly if you feel you are being treated unacceptably. Don't be afraid to discuss the matter with the biological parent, and draw up a plan together for dealing with such incidents in the future.

Every time my child spends a weekend with his non-resident parent he is upset and difficult when he comes home.

Although such situations are common, they are not inevitable, so assume that something can be done to improve things. Children can sometimes feel insecure when they spend time with a non-resident parent they don't see often, and may try to test out whether they can push you away too by behaving in a challenging manner once they get home.

Seeing the absent parent may also revive a child's old resentment that the parents no longer live together, so you may be blamed for disrupting the old status quo, or even find yourself on the receiving end of displaced anger that your child feels towards the absent parent. If any of these is the case, a frank conversation with your child and the necessary reassurance may be enough to settle him down.

Sometimes a child may act up simply because routines have been disrupted, or because he's having to cope with a very different parenting style and expectations. In the worst-case scenario, perhaps the non-resident parent has sought to make an alliance with the child against you. To avoid this it is important to maintain a reasonable working relationship with your ex-partner, based upon making the children's best interests the first priority at all times.

I can't get my ex-partner to take responsibility for our children.

It is a sad fact that while your ex-partner can be pursued through the courts to make financial provision for your children, there is no way to ensure that any other responsibilities are fulfilled. If the absent parent is not sufficiently motivated to stay in touch and take an interest, it is probably not in your child's interest to force the issue as you may be setting her up for a series of rejections and disappointments. If you have sincerely tried and failed to engage the non-resident parent, it could well be better to cut your losses, entertain minimal expectations of that person and prepare yourself for some painful discussions with your child about why the absent parent is showing so little commitment.

My child refuses to do what I tell her.

If this is consistently the case, you have probably got yourself into a power struggle in which the issue of control has become paramount for both sides. Try to make sure that communicating with your child consists of more than a string of commands and instructions, and use negotiating strategies with older children when you can: for example, 'You can go out and see your friends if you tidy your room.' Where you can, offer choices between acceptable options so that your child retains some sense of control: 'Do you want to unload the dishwasher or help Dad to hang out the washing?'

When a child constantly refuses to do what you ask, you may just have to endure some temporary emotional fireworks while you hold your nerve. After a single warning, use consequences such as 'time out' – a brief spell away from the fray, where your child can calm down and 'start again' without loss of face – or the removal of a privilege instead of raising your voice. This is a very effective strategy, but you have to stay calm, be consistent and get ready for a long period of readjustment, during which your child will push you to your limits to see if you really mean business.

I don't like my child's friends.

Fortunately, they are not *your* friends, so you don't have to like them. However, as they are likely to be visitors in your home from time to time, you are perfectly within your rights to insist upon acceptable standards of behaviour while they are under your roof. If they cannot treat your home respectfully, perhaps stop the visits.

If you are seriously worried about the influence an older child's friends are having on him, you should express your concerns and point out what you see as the potential consequences of the friendship, but acknowledge that you cannot ultimately control whom he chooses to mix with. You might like to express your faith that he will handle himself and his relationships in a responsible manner. Remember, none of us likes it when others criticize people we are fond of, and if your child is vulnerable to the influence of others, it is important not to alienate him at this crucial stage.

I am worried that my child is taking drugs.

This is a common fear and the subject needs to be be treated with sensitivity. Rather than spying on your child or going through her possessions in search of evidence, try to have a face-to-face conversation. If you are seriously concerned and have evidence to substantiate your fears, you must tell your child, but first consult websites such as www.talktofrank.com, which offers advice for parents and has a twenty-four-hour helpline number.

Moving on

'Without a family, man, alone in the world, trembles with the cold,' according to the novelist André Malraux (1901–76). I agree! But it is very hard work, and we have only just begun, because in the next chapter we look at things from the child's point of view.

CHAPTER 6 Children Growing Up

Our birth is but a sleep and a forgetting;
The soul that rises with us, our life's star,
Hath had elsewhere its setting,
And cometh from afar:
Not in entire forgetfulness,
And not in utter nakedness,
But trailing clouds of glory do we come
From God who is our home;
Heaven lies about us in our infancy!

William Wordsworth (1770–1850)
'Intimations of Immortality from Recollections
of Early Childhood'

Blink and children seem to have grown several centimetres. The infants who were once crawling are suddenly running around. No sooner have they started school than they are off to university. It all happens so fast that you may hardly have considered how it feels from your children's point of view. Perhaps these questions will give you pause for thought.

- What do you think of children today?
- What can you remember about your own childhood?
- What do you enjoy most about your children?
- What are your children good at?
- How is your child changing at the moment?
- What challenges you most about the way your child gets on with you and with others?
- What challenges you most about the way your children get on with each other?

- If you have stepchildren, what particular opportunities and challenges do they bring?
- If children are growing up with one parent only, what particular opportunities and challenges do you think this brings?

As your answers to these questions probably indicate, being a parent today is hard, but so is being a child.

The pressures on children are immense. They live in increasingly complex family structures. At the click of a button they can see cultural diversity that ranges from North American affluence to African famine. In the Western world the education system puts them under enormous pressure to succeed academically, with regular testing and examinations to record their progress. For some the pressure is simply too much to bear. Sometimes the heavenly excitement of childhood to which Wordsworth alludes seems almost unbelievable.

Where is the family in all of this? How do families address wider social issues these days? It is no longer as straightforward as it used to be. What kind of role models and expectations are established within today's families? Do we teach our children to believe what the media says or do we challenge these views? How can we encourage children to think and feel for themselves? How do we deal with the different views our children encounter in their friends and at school? How easy is it for children to talk to us about these things? What if they don't want to talk? Are there other responsible adults they can trust, who have their best interests at heart, and to whom they can talk freely?

And where do we get our information about children? If it comes mostly from adults, can we trust it? Are our own memories of childhood still reliable within today's world? Can we make sense of what our children tell us about their lives, and how much should we be swayed by their concerns?

There are no simple answers to any of these questions, but this chapter tries to offer some insights. We will be trying to understand what is going on for children as they grow from babies to teenagers, and how they interact with each other and with the adults around them.

Making comparisons

One of the most powerful concerns for any parent is the nagging question 'Is my child normal?' Privately, we all want the answer to be 'Better than normal', but that, of course, is impossible. Normality does not work as a mathematical concept (some children would have to be 'better' and some would have to be 'worse' for the sums to add up), and when you look at what is happening to children as they grow up, you realize that it is just not that simple (children develop in very different ways, depending on a host of complex factors).

This is the moment in *Happy Families* when you might expect to find a chart showing what you should expect your child to be able to do at different ages. But as there are plenty of books and websites where you can find such things, I am not going to include one here. I find that charts tend to induce unnecessary paranoia among parents, who immediately start worrying that their child does not seem able to do something that other 'normal' children of the same age can do.

However, you might be interested in finding out a little more about the general phases of development you can expect your child to go through as he or she grows up.

Key developments

The first person to attempt to describe the key stages of child development was Swiss psychologist Jean Piaget. Through observation of children, Piaget suggested that there are four main stages.

Ages 0–2: Sensory-motor
Children recognize objects as being different from themselves and start deciding what to do or not do (for example, to hold a ball rather than a toothbrush).

Ages 2–7: Pre-operational
Children begin to use language, although they can use only crude categories to describe objects, being mainly interested in what things look like rather than what they are used for. Anything round, for example, may called a 'ball'. Children are still very much self-centred.

Ages 7–11: Concrete operational
Children begin to be more subtle in their categorization of objects. So, for example, a child can understand that water can exist as rain, or in a bottle, or coming out of a tap. They can use numbers and can also think logically about people and events.

Age 11+: Formal operational
Children can begin to think more abstractly, so the big questions of existence ('Who am I?' 'What is the meaning of life?') can begin to be explored.

You can see how influential Piaget's ideas have been when you look at our school system, which uses ages seven and eleven as key points for tests, and often makes eleven the age for moving on to a secondary school.

But Piaget's ideas focus mainly on one aspect of a child's development – the development of thinking – and assume that this takes place largely in isolation from other children and adults. Nowadays we do not believe that these four stages are as clear or rigid as Piaget implies.

Other people take very different approaches to child development. They explore the social situation in which children develop (the importance of friends, for example); or they seek to understand the role of the community in which children grow up; or they look at the development of emotions (remember the attachment theory discussed on pages 57–9). And some challenge the idea that very young children are not capable of sophisticated thoughts or emotions.

At the heart of all questions about development is the nature versus nurture debate: are we born 'programmed' to be a certain kind of person or do we learn to be who we are as we grow up? The anser is almost certainly a combination of the two, but while it is important for parents to understand those things that may be hardwired into their child and contribute to his unique personality, it is more important still to see and accept their influential role in helping their child to develop and grow.

Family life cycles

As well as understanding more about children as individuals, it is also useful to think about some of the ways in which the nuclear family (mum, dad and children) goes through cycles at different ages. A family with three children under five, for example, will function very differently from one with two teenage girls or one that has two children from one relationship and two of similar ages from another. A family with young children at primary school and an older child at secondary school will sometimes seem to inhabit two worlds. Parents will be talking about adult things with the teenager that they might not want to discuss with the younger children. Two 'levels' of activities will therefore need to be on offer for the period during which the children are at home. This will present particular challenges when it comes to selecting family holidays.

The birth of children inevitably puts strain on parents. Priorities have to change dramatically if the new family is to be happy and prosper. But what about when children leave the home? Things may have changed in the post-nuclear family but the departure of the children is still likely to be a significant step that will require adjustment for all concerned. It's sometimes called empty-nest syndrome, and can be a challenging time for parents who have to readjust to living their lives for each other without the presence (and sometimes excuse) of the children. Interestingly, for many people, especially women, this may be a time of considerable liberation.

Another trend in modern family life is for older children to remain at home after they have finished their education. Usually this happens for financial reasons – debts after university – but sometimes it can be because parents have become too dependent on their children and vice versa. Does there come a time when you need to ask your child to move out of the family nest? If your child lives with you beyond a certain age, does she become a lodger (with attendant rights and responsibilities)? Should she pay rent?

And the role of grandparents is changing too. In our increasingly ageing society, grandparents are more likely to be fit and healthy enough to help with childcare. But equally, they may want to explore their own life, travelling and socializing with friends now that they are freed from the demands of work.

Introducing a new baby

It's one thing to be a parent to a lone child, but a whole new ball game when it comes to dealing with two or more. Everything is much more complex and, of course, the children may not get on with each other. The literature of families, from *King Lear* to *Cinderella*, is full of sibling rivalry and the unhappiness that it can cause. Are there ways in which you can ensure that your children will get on with each other? Let's take a moment to explore these issues.

Introducing a new baby to older children is something that many parents have to go through. While there is no single way of doing this effectively, it is clear that some approaches seem to work better than others. We also know from research that dealing with the feelings of your first-born child or older children is very important and can shape their reaction to the new arrival.

How to introduce a new child

If you are about to have a baby, you might like to think about the following topics.

When to tell your child
There is no right time. But remember that once you have told your child, the arrival of a baby will seldom be far from her mind. And even if the baby is not due for ages, a young child has little idea of time, so may well assume that the new baby will arrive 'tomorrow'.

You might want to link the date to something she will grasp, such as Christmas or a holiday. Try to pick a moment to talk when you will not be interrupted, have plenty of time and are all feeling relaxed and comfortable.

How to talk about it
Children are all different: some will want to talk about the new baby all the time, while others may prefer to ask the occasional question. You need to be sensitive to your own child. Reading books about the experience of introducing a new brother or sister is also helpful (see pages 211–13).

Sharing your love
Children often worry that the new baby will take away your love for them, or that there will not be enough love to go around. This is often the case if the older child is of primary school age, where the concept of division is beginning to have some meaning. You can help your child to see that love cannot be subtracted by pointing out that he doesn't stop loving one of his parents when both parents are in the room. You can also explain that love is a magic substance that keeps growing, so there is always enough to go around.

Involving your child
As the birth approaches, think through how you can make sure your child is as involved as possible in the arrival of the baby. In many cases there will be a period when the mother is not available because she is in hospital. Making sure that your child does not feel abandoned and is being looked after and made to feel special is important. Typically, this could be done by a close relative, who might also bring the child to the hospital (unless the father can do this). At the moment of first meeting, it is helpful if the mother can make sure that she is available to hug the child as a priority rather than occupied with the baby. Then, as family and friends gradually come to see the new arrival, ask them to make a point of saying hello to your older child or children before oohing and aahing over the baby. Developing the role of the oldest sibling and allowing your child to share in some of the practical responsibilities of looking after the new baby can also ease potential rivalry.

The first few weeks are really important in establishing a good relationship between your older child(ren) and a new baby. But even if all goes really well, you may still have to deal with sibling jealousy and rivalry, in which case you may find it helpful to use some of the techniques described on pages 151–2.

Happy blended families

The present-day trend towards divorce and multiple partners means that families containing stepchildren are a growing phenomenon. Unfortunately, the arrival of stepchildren can be even more traumatic for your existing child than the planned arrival of a new baby.

Blending a family created from different relationships is hard work. Children may still be dealing with the 'loss' of a parent and be jealous of stepsiblings, but it *is* possible to create a happily blended family. Much depends on two things: the attitude of the step-parent and the sensitivity with which he or she plays this role, and the attitude of the other biological parent. If the non-resident parent is angry and negative towards the step-parent who is spending time with their children, this can cause difficulties.

Given time, many stepchildren become firm friends. But if your children are not getting on well, or you are experiencing sibling rivalries at the moment, you might like to read the troubleshooting section for more advice on what to do (see page 164).

Five principles for raising happy children

You cannot guarantee that your children will grow up happily, but if you adopt the following five principles, there is a good chance that they (and you) will be happy.

Principle 1: Treat your child as an individual

Once upon a time, childhood was considered to be little more than an unfortunate period between birth and young adulthood. Children were assumed to have general needs – for food, shelter and a certain amount of love – but these needs were seldom personalized. Now we know better. We know that being treated as an individual from an early age is really important for happiness and well-being.

From the earliest days it is possible to see your child's individuality. A famous study of children's temperament carried out by Stella Chess and Alexander Thomas in the 1950s found that children fell into three main categories: easy, difficult and slow to warm up. Note, however, that this study was dealing with difficult children and that it is always important to be wary of labelling children.

Easy children have regular eating and sleeping cycles, and respond positively to new situations. They quickly adapt to changes, such as different food or a new school. They are in a good mood most of the time and smile often.

Difficult children have irregular eating and sleeping cycles. They tend to respond negatively to new situations, perhaps by crying or having tantrums. They are slow to adapt to change, and need more time to get used to new food or new people.

Slow-to-warm-up children have some difficulty with new situations, and their reactions are much less intense than in the other two categories of children.

Chess and Thomas's work gave a biological basis to the individual temperament with which we are born. It showed that if children from each of these different categories were treated in ways sensitive to their temperament, they were more likely to thrive. They called this 'goodness of fit' (as opposed to 'poorness of fit').

In the next few pages I want to explore the ways in which parents can find out more about children and nurture their individuality.

Think about individuality

Take a moment to think about each one of your children in turn. Use these questions to prompt you to think about them as individuals.

- Which of the categories above would you put your child in? (If none of them seems quite right, an approximation is fine.)
- What is most important to your child at the moment?
- What does your child enjoy doing most?
- What does your child enjoy doing least?
- What irritates your child most?
- Who is the most important person in your child's life (other than parents)?
- Name your child's three closest friends.
- What does your child worry about most?
- Does your child have any enemies? If so, who are they?
- Who are your child's favourite authors? What are her favourite films? Favourite TV programmes? Favourite music? Favourite clothes? Favourite places? Most important hobbies?
- Which people does your child most admire?

Did you find these questions easy or hard to answer? If you found them difficult, it might be worth spending some time observing and listening to your child very carefully. Assuming that you managed to answer a fair few of them, what next? What can you do that will help you to treat your child as an individual and thus help him to be happier?

There are really two aspects to this. First, you need to know your child (as the questions above have already indicated). Second, you might like to do things that are likely to help him develop his individuality. See the suggestions in the box below.

How to encourage individuality

1. Take your child to the library from an early age and encourage him to read widely. Make sure that you show your own interest in reading and that you read to him too.

2. Take your child to visit as many different interesting places and performances as possible – museums, historic houses, farms, gardens, sporting events, concerts, etc.

3. Notice what your child is currently interested in and get hold of posters for the bedroom or interesting DVDs or computer programs.

4. Limit the amount of time children spend in front of the television or playing computer games (see Troubleshooting on page 164 for more guidance on this).

5. Listen to your child talking and use this to glean clues about what she is interested in. Ask good questions (requiring more than 'yes' or 'no' answers) about her interests.

6. Introduce your child to new people. You might like to invite some of your adult friends to supper occasionally so that your child can take part in conversations with them.

7. Find a mentor for your child to act as a role model and help develop his talents. This might be a mature teenager, or perhaps a young adult with some similar interests.

8. Talk to your children. Consciously use new words to help develop their vocabulary.

9. Play games together, especially those that require conversation and thinking and do not just depend on luck.

The individuality of intelligence

For a long time the only measure of a child's talent was IQ (intelligence quotient). This is a score from a standardized test that attempts to measure a person's thinking abilities in relation to their age group. An IQ test assumes an average of 100, so a score of 120 is 'above average' and ninety is 'below average'.

At one time it was thought that being clever was all about having a high IQ. Now we realize that intelligence is much more complex than this. Indeed, American professor of education Howard Gardner has suggested that we have not one, but multiple intelligences – eight in fact. These are:

- linguistic
- logical-mathematical
- musical
- naturalist
- spatial
- bodily kinaesthetic
- interpersonal
- intrapersonal

Most of these terms are fairly self-explanatory. Kinaesthetic relates to awareness of the body's muscles, and the last two refer, respectively, to the ability to make sense of relationships and the ability to make sense of and manage emotions. Whether you agree with Gardner's views of multiple intelligence or not (and not everyone does), his view of talent is a very attractive one. For if you adopt his approach, the role of parents (and teachers and anyone else interested in promoting the development of young people) becomes one of talent-spotter and encourager, constantly on the lookout for areas where a child may be able to succeed.

It also takes the focus away from assessing talent only in terms of academic success, and moves you into thinking about how you can help your child become an effective lifelong learner. (See also Chapter 8.)

According to an African proverb, 'It takes a village to bring up a child'. If you really want to develop your child's full range of talents, you may want to remember these words, for it will take the resources of many people other than you and your partner to accomplish this.

Principle 2: Share your love equally

After the emphasis on individuality in the first principle, it may at first seem odd to be talking about equality of treatment if we are all different. But sharing your love equally does not necessarily mean treating everyone in the family identically.

The point is that everyone has to get enough of what they need. A loving relationship will recognize that the balance of every individual's needs is unique. Some children may require more attention than others. Some children may genuinely prefer not to be fussed over too much. Your role as a parent is to find out what works for your children and give them what really counts.

But if you have ever been in a situation where one child is clearly being favoured above others, you will know just how corrosive this can be. It can breed resentment and lead to terrible sibling jealousy, especially when the adult is no longer in the room. As Mother Teresa (1910–97) once put it, 'There is more hunger for love and appreciation in this world than for bread'. And where there is unsatisfied hunger, powerful needs are created.

Conversely, when you walk into a home where the parents clearly love all their children equally, stepchildren or otherwise, the environment feels warm and encouraging, ideal for bringing up a happy family.

You can see this in a number of ways that you might want to imitate.

Differences are celebrated. When love is shared equally, being different is seen as something special rather than odd. As a parent, you can show this in the way you speak about those close to you, always commenting positively on their unique talents – 'You're so good at noticing beetles'; 'You really seemed to enjoy watching cricket today'; 'Dad's so good at cooking' – rather than drawing attention to differences in a negative way – 'She has a really high-pitched voice'; 'I'm glad I'm not like him'. Loving people equally implies that you spend equal time looking for what is special in everyone. This is particularly important in a society where being the same as other people is apparently valued so highly that you are not cool unless you are wearing the same clothes, watching the same films and listening to the same music as everyone else.

Stereotypes are avoided. 'That's typical of a girl.' 'Only a boy would do that.' 'Children like you do this or don't do this…' It's so easy to fall into the stereotype trap. Our brains make assumptions about the way people are and how they are likely to behave, often based on inadequate data or on what other people have told us. Myths are perpetuated. Children (and adults) get hurt. And this immediately undermines any attempts you may be making to celebrate differences.
So try to avoid falling into this trap, and challenge stereotypes whenever anyone in your family uses one.

Comparisons are avoided. While it is almost impossible to stop yourself from comparing your children, try to keep these comparisons safe inside your head. It may be tempting to tell your daughter that she is tidier than your son, or remark that one child reads better than another, but such comments can easily turn into putdowns, so are best avoided. In most families children will each have different strengths and weaknesses. When the differences are very obvious, and especially if one child is conspicuously more successful at school, sport or music, you might need to work particularly hard to ensure that you avoid comparisons that could undermine any 'weaker' child.

Children are treated fairly. It goes without saying that children need to be treated fairly, and that this is an obvious indicator of the even-handedness of your love. But it does not always mean that you have to treat your children identically. Children of very different ages require different treatment, but they all have long memories (about bedtimes, for example) and will brood on apparent inequities. All rules get bent in busy families, but if complaints arise, you must be seen to handle them fairly.

Personal space

If you live in a flat or a small house, it may be very difficult to allocate some personal space for everyone, but it is important to try. If your children are to develop their individual talents and temperaments, it is important that they can create a mini-environment that reflects their personality. It might be just part of a bedroom wall, or a particular shelf. However small the space, it is helpful for each of your children to have somewhere that they can call their own. (See more about this in Chapter 7.)

Of course, the simplest way of all to ensure that your children experience your love equally is to make a point of telling each one that he or she is special (and some of the reasons why) at least once a week.

Principle 3: Build children's esteem

The idea of self-esteem is something that has fascinated researchers for at least a century. Self-esteem, like its close cousin self-confidence, is a mysterious thing, perhaps best summed up as 'how you feel about yourself'. It is a fascinating area because it is so complex. What makes *you* feel good about yourself may not work for *me*. Where you might feel good after giving what you think was a good speech, I might feel bad because I think it could have gone so much better.

Helping your child to develop positive self-esteem is, for me, the most important principle in this chapter, and the one to which all the others are connected in some way. There are lots of things you can do to help your child achieve self-esteem, but you cannot hand it to her on a plate, and it does not derive from simply telling her that she has it.

Ingredients of self-esteem

By common consent among psychologists, there seem to be three principle ingredients in self-esteem.

1. A sense of who you are (how comfortable you are with your strengths, weaknesses, individual characteristics and appearance).

2. A sense of how you belong (that you are happy to be in relationships with other people, and feel loved and valued).

3. A sense of your own personal power (your inner knowledge that you can cope with things and make a difference in life).

It seems that babies are born with enough self-esteem, but as time goes by, they either feel positive about themselves or struggle to do so. Young children pick up on what others around them appear to value, especially their parents, and if they feel that they cannot succeed in these areas, they may develop low self-esteem.

In *Happy Families* you have already learnt about many of the things that are important in nurturing self-esteem, such as being positive, setting goals, understanding yourself and others, developing individuality and surrounding your children with love. But there are some further things that you can do.

Help children to be comfortable with themselves

If you want your child to be comfortable with himself, a good starting point is yourself. If you provide a positive, confident role model, someone who is clearly at ease with who you are and not always complaining about the things you would like to change about yourself or others, your child will see this and be influenced by it.

The diarist Anne Frank (1929–45), wise beyond her years, wrote in her wartime diary: 'I tell myself time and time again to overlook mother's bad example. I only want to see her good points, and to look inside myself for what is lacking in her. But it doesn't work.'

Parental example is a powerful thing, but it can be hard to project a positive image if you are going through a tough time, such as the break-up of a relationship or a radical change of direction in your career. In such situations, being able to call on the support of close friends can help, and it might also be useful to find some kind of parenting support group. When you are feeling low, it is important to do some things for yourself to ensure that you keep your own sense of self-worth intact and can thus be a more positive parent for your child.

Times of challenge

There are, of course, key moments for your children when their self-esteem may be challenged. These include going to school for the first time, moving on from primary school, dealing with the arrival of a new sibling and coping with a change in their parents' relationship.

Perhaps most challenging, though, are the teenage years, when rapid emotional, physical and intellectual changes force young people to rethink who they are. In its extreme form, such self-analysis can lead to depression, eating disorders and feelings of self-loathing, so it is important for parents to be aware of what adolescence may bring. Trying to increase your understanding of teenage culture, finding out about some of the biological changes that occur and talking to parents who have gone through the teenage years may be helpful. At this stage of your child's life it will be important for you to learn the gentle art of 'letting go', allowing your teenagers to develop autonomy and accepting that their friends are going to become more important to them in this phase than their family. You should not be offended if they don't want to participate in family life in the same way as previously.

A counter view to this is provided in a recent book by Penny Palamano called *Yes, Please, Whatever!* She argues that, despite their age and size, teenagers should be treated as if they are 'tall toddlers' because their brain is not completely developed and they are unlikely to be able to prioritize or control their emotions. She therefore advocates a much more hands-on approach, which is summarized in the following list.

Dos and don'ts of parenting children

- Dress your age.
- Do not talk 'hip'.
- Don't kiss your teenagers in front of their friends.
- Don't show photos of them to their friends.
- Do not swear.
- Don't drink too much.
- Don't make jokes about sex.
- Don't kiss your partner in their presence.
- Don't try to be cool in front of their friends.

There's a lot of sense in this list, but I completely disagree with her points about public displays of affection. It is, in fact, quite possible to surround your children with displays of physical affection from an early age in such a way that, as most Continental parents know, hugging is seen as normal rather than odd.

When parenting teenagers, the goal remains much as it has always been: to have a strong, loving and trusting relationship with your offspring so that they will continue to be open with you, talk to you and listen to your advice. Teenagers might appear not to be listening to you, but they often are (even if you have to repeat things several times).

Helping your child to belong

From the word go you can help your child to have a strong sense of belonging. This is achieved mainly by your consistent and unwavering display of love.

You can convince your child that she is surrounded by people who care about her and think well of her by the way you talk to her and about her. You can make sure that in any typical day you praise your child (genuinely) for the good things she does. You can also restrict your criticism to things that really matter, so adverse comments happen much less frequently than praise.

You can ensure that your child knows all about your family and her place in it. A good way of reinforcing this is to make sure there are lots of photographs around the house that show close friends and family doing things together and clearly enjoying them. Home videos or DVDs can serve a positive role here; just don't inflict them on people outside the family.

As your child grows up, you can encourage her to be better at describing the things she is good at. If you have clearly noticed and commented on improvements over time, this will make her self-assessment much easier (see pages 114–18).

As you realize more about your child's developing identity, you can look out for opportunities for her to become involved in local groups that will enable her to see and hear things about herself that will further strengthen the growing sense of her own value and talents.

Within the family, the more you can show that you expect each member to be cooperative and look out for the others, the better. This will embed in a child's mind the idea that not only does she belong, but so does everyone else in her immediate world.

As well as celebrating your child's successes, it's a good idea to celebrate some of the milestones in her life, such as the first day of not wearing a nappy, going to school for the first time, walking back from school alone, and becoming a teenager. Celebrating and marking such events provides an additional level of comfort and belonging for your child.

Keeping a scrapbook, making a family photo album, collecting photos of your relations, even trying to work out your family tree can all be means of providing more concrete reminders of the way in which your child (and you) belong to a bigger family.

In addition, being part of a church or other faith 'family' provides a powerful way of helping your child to develop a sense of belonging.

Helping your child to develop personal power

Self-esteem is most challenged when you meet a situation that you seem not to be able to deal with. If you feel that you have somehow failed to grapple with it, and especially if this goes on happening, it is easy to begin to doubt your own capabilities.

As a parent wanting to give your child the gift of personal happiness, you have a responsibility to help him develop the kind of emotional and social skills that will enable him to use his own personal power. By 'personal power' I mean the capacity to stick up for yourself (without being aggressive), believe in yourself and take responsibility for sorting things out when you need to. Without this core inner strength, it will be all too easy for your child to give in to circumstances and find himself doing things that he does not really want to do. This can lead to all sorts of negative feelings and difficult situations.

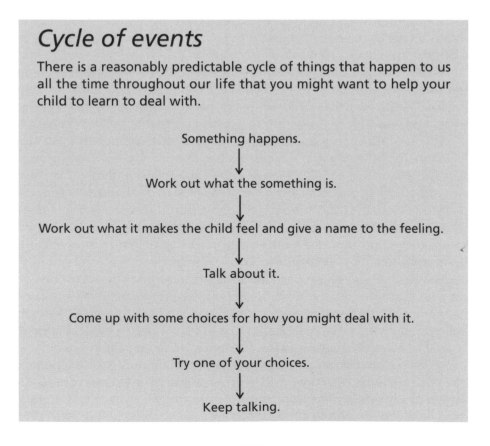

Cycle of events

There is a reasonably predictable cycle of things that happen to us all the time throughout our life that you might want to help your child to learn to deal with.

Something happens.
↓
Work out what the something is.
↓
Work out what it makes the child feel and give a name to the feeling.
↓
Talk about it.
↓
Come up with some choices for how you might deal with it.
↓
Try one of your choices.
↓
Keep talking.

At every stage of this process you can help your child. In Troubleshooting on page 164 you can see how you might deal with some of the more challenging situations that can arise for parents. (You might want to remind yourself about how to be a parent/coach by looking at page 125 again.)

In essence, exercising personal power involves learning how to take responsibility for your feelings so that, however awful the situation in which you find yourself, you can talk about it and take action to change things. Having personal power means that claims such as 'He made me do it' stop meaning anything. People can't make you do things, except in times of war and certain tragic personal circumstances. You can say no. You can walk away. You can come up with a response that works for you.

And you, as the parent, can help your child to develop personal power by supporting him as he develops the skills that go with each stage of the process outlined on page 156. It need not be as mechanistic as this might imply, but can be fun, with lots of safe exploration together about situations that may occur, and role play to explore how you might deal with them.

Principle 4: Provide a challenging but secure environment

As well as making sure that your child feels secure – loved and with high self-esteem – you also need to provide for another basic human need: the desire to explore and challenge. As personal growth expert John Bradshaw puts it: 'Children are curious and are risk-takers. They have lots of courage. They venture out into a world that is immense and dangerous. A child initially trusts life and the processes of life.'

As a parent you need to provide an environment in which your child can explore things safely before he or she ventures out into the world, for challenge is essential to growth and enriches the young mind. Children are full of questions. 'What does this do?' 'How does that work?' 'Why are there so many of these?' And the more you can provide an environment in which questions are encouraged, the longer your child will maintain the sense of curiosity that is so central to being an effective learner.

Wherever possible, you want your children to work things out for themselves. This way they will stay motivated. Children tend to respond well to challenge, provided it does not push them too far. A challenge is an invitation to 'stretch' yourself. Challenge is essential in learning: it stimulates you to develop and gets you motivated. When this happens your brain literally changes its chemistry. (Your neurons are stimulated into growing more dendrites so that they can connect with other neurons, and your brain's capacity is thus expanded.)

But with challenge there is a tipping point. Too much pressure can easily create an unhelpfully stressful situation in which it is difficult to maintain motivation. The impact of stress and challenge on your child's motivation works like this:

	High stress	Low stress
High challenge	Feels controlled and compelled	Feels engaged
Low challenge	Feels controlled and demotivated	Feels bored

Children feel engaged when they are asked to do something at the edge of their competence and rise to the occasion. If it is too easy, they get bored. But if they are put under too much pressure, they may end up feeling used and controlled. This is also true for adults.

Your goal as a parent is to encourage your child to be resilient and develop staying power. This means constantly helping your child to go to the next step.

Russian psychologist Lev Vygotsky was the first to explain how adults could help children to do this. Unlike Piaget, whose ideas you met on page 143, Vygotsky saw the development of children as fundamentally a social activity involving interaction with their peers and, most importantly, with key adults. He came up with a simple but powerful idea – the 'zone of proximal development'. This refers to the immediate next step your child can take – something that is just beyond what he is currently comfortable with. The role of the adult is to spot this point and help the child to try out something that will stretch him just beyond his current capability. By doing this you are helping your child to become a 'stronger' learner by exercising his 'learning muscles'.

For the learner to succeed in the zone of proximal development, he has to be prepared to come out of his comfort zone. The role of those helping the learner is to provide support or 'scaffolding' to help him get from where he is now to where he wants to go. Vygotsky's thinking provides the clearest possible rationale for parents to be coaches, constantly looking for what might be the next challenge for their child and always thinking about the kind of support they can provide.

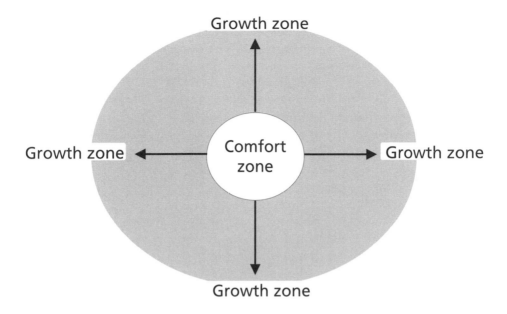

Take the example of a parent teaching a child how to ride a bike. Let's assume that your child starts out with stabilizers. Then one day she gets up enough confidence to sit on the saddle while you hold the bike and walk alongside. After a while, sitting on the bike and being pushed by you becomes relatively easy – a comfort zone.

If you want your child to learn how to ride unaided, you will have to encourage her to try it for a few metres on her own (preferably on a soft surface, such as grass). The first time a child does this it is scary but exhilarating. Gradually the child will go further, each time being encouraged by you, until suddenly she's 'got it'. This is Vygotsky's theory in action. It applies just as well to helping a child learn how to sit up in a bath without support, how to dress himself, how to read, how to walk to the local shop on his own and so forth.

The parental role is crucial in judging how much support and how much challenge the child can cope with. Of course, children will make mistakes, and there is a great temptation for parents to see this as failure and for the child to get downhearted. But if you want your child to become a resilient person, you need him to make mistakes and learn from them. How can you learn to do without a nappy unless at some time you have felt the sensation of warm pee on your leg and marvelled at the pool of yellow water at your feet? How can you learn to buy a few items at your local shop unless you make the odd mistake and come back with something that is close to what your parents asked you to get, but not quite right? Effective parents know the developmental value of mistakes and encourage their children to make them while in the secure environment of their home. When you are at the edge of what you feel confident about, of course you are likely to make mistakes. That's how you learn to do better next time.

Inevitably, children's mistakes can be messy in the home: paint on the carpet, a broken family heirloom... One practical suggestion to reduce the number of times you feel the need to say things such as 'Not there, please' and 'Don't touch that, please' is to create a small area of your home, ideally with a washable floor – perhaps a corner of your kitchen – where the children can make a mess that is easy to clear up.

A word of warning. It can be tempting to take Vygotsky's ideas too far and create a sort of hothouse environment in the hope that you can turn your child into a genius. Indeed, you may be persuaded by commercial products, such as flashcards and classical music tapes, that this is possible. While there is nothing wrong with parents helping a child to read or encouraging an interest in Mozart, putting too much emphasis on accelerating the development of your child can be counter-productive. In fact, the education system puts children under enormous pressure already, and they need to know that home is somewhere they can relax as well as learn.

Perhaps more importantly, there is no evidence that this kind of accelerated learning actually lasts. While you may get some immediate gains, research has shown that after a few years there is little or no difference in children's attainment. Worst of all, you might just kill off your child's natural curiosity along the way if you try to over-regiment her early learning. (You can read more about what you can helpfully do at home to aid learning in Chapter 7.)

A second word of warning concerns your relationship with your child. As she grows up and you encourage her to rise to new challenges, you are likely to become close. If you encourage your child to talk openly to you, it is likely that she will share confidences about herself and about the choices she is facing. This is healthy and good, but there is a kind of tipping point that you might like to watch out for. It's the moment when you catch yourself beginning to play the role of friend rather than parent. You can so successfully put yourself in your child's shoes that you are almost thinking like her. This is not what your child needs. You need to be a consistently approachable and reliable parent rather than a best friend. If you get too close, it becomes much more difficult to ensure that there are proper boundaries beyond which your child cannot go.

Principle 5: Teach children how to behave

The principles so far have focused very much on love and support, but you must also be aware that you have some other parental responsibilities that must be fulfilled if you and your children are going to be truly happy. I'm alluding in particular to the 'd' word: discipline. You need to teach your child how to behave.

Can discipline and happy family life go together? Most definitely. In fact, without discipline it is unlikely that your family will be happy. Perhaps some of you will protest that discipline is just a way of trying to enforce adult superiority and has no place in today's freer society. That's simply wrong. Discipline should be seen as structured, systematic and careful teaching of your child in ways that are appropriate to him or her as an individual.

Of course, parents have many different approaches to disciplining their children. It can involve mentoring, setting up situations where children can see clear and unambiguous connections between their own actions and their consequences, sometimes having the courage to stand back and let children make mistakes, and thus equipping them with the skills they need for life.

Discipline can also be about role modelling, showing children what to do. This could include demonstrating how to be assertive in the face of difficult behaviour. Showing how we ourselves draw boundaries and stipulate conditions – perhaps walking away and disengaging if our children talk abusively to us – is a good example.

Discipline can also be part of socialization, teaching children how their actions impact on others and fostering the development of empathy and social skills. This will allow them to fit into the wider system outside the family and to make it work for them.

Discipline can be soft or hard. It can rely mainly on praise with occasional critical comments, or be constantly telling children off. There are as many different views about what discipline is as there are parents.

What's your view on discipline?

Take a moment to think about your own approach to discipline.

▷ What are you trying to achieve? (You could look back at the parent roles on pages 102–13 to stimulate your thinking.)

▷ What are the values underlying what you are doing and where do they come from?

In practice in most happy households, discipline involves setting and keeping to a relatively small number of clear expectations. Sometimes these are moral values (such as never using any form of violence); sometimes they are ethical ones (such as always sharing whatever you have); and often they are practical ones (such as not getting down from the table until everyone has finished eating).

From the child's point of view, these are the boundaries – the rules of the game of life – in your home. All children need rules and expectations to help them learn appropriate behaviour. It is important to view discipline as teaching rather than punishment. Learning to follow rules keeps children safe and helps them to learn the difference between right and wrong. It is your primary means of sharing your values with them.

So how do you teach a child your rules, and what should you do when those rules are broken? Do you reason with a misbehaving child? Do you threaten him? Do you hit him? Do you ignore him, hoping that the behaviour will stop of its own accord? Do you banish him to his room? Do you get help from the other parent or another carer? Most parents have done most of these things (or at least felt like doing them) at some time in their life.

Try not to respond in the heat of the moment. Find some time of adult calmness with your partner or a close friend to talk about what the rules are and how you want to handle discipline in your home. There are many options.

Tips for dealing with discipline

Look at the following tips and see if you can adapt them to your own personal circumstances. Although they look straightforward enough on the printed page, they need constant practice and adaptation until you feel confident that they work for you.

Catch your child being successful.
Positive mindsets have been a feature of *Happy Families* and are very important if you want to ensure that your discipline is more about teaching than about punishment. Praising your child for not doing things that he sometimes does ('Well done for staying so calm'; 'I really like the way you waited patiently for the rest of us to finish eating') is a powerful means of surrounding him with your rules in a wholly positive way. It's a great idea to use a digital camera to capture 'good behaviour', which can then be pinned up on a notice-board as a visual reminder to all concerned. Children love watching the pictures develop, and as they do so, the positive messages are reinforced.

Show trust.
If rules become a way of catching your child out, they are likely to be a cause of strife. But if the assumption in your home is that everyone trusts everyone else to do what they say they will, there can be two very helpful side-effects. The first is that your child is likely to feel good about being treated in an adult way. The second is that you will often have to rehearse situations before they happen so your rule will be uppermost in your child's head. Thus, if your rule is that your child needs to be back home by a certain time, you could say, 'Just talk me through what time you are planning to leave your friend's house', or 'What time did you say the bus leaves? Do you think you've left yourself enough time to get there?'

Be firm, reasonable and calm.
When children get emotional about something, they often do not hear what you are saying. And the more heated you get, the more the situation is likely to escalate. So it is really important for you to be firm ('Please turn the television off now'), reasonable ('I want you to be back here by 6 p.m. before it gets dark' or 'If you do that again, I am going to stop playing with you'), and calm (try to slow down as you speak). Sometimes taking a minute's 'time out' (removing the child or asking him to leave the room for a few moments' breather) is all that is needed to restore calm.

Provide a diversion.
When children misbehave you often need not a sanction but a diversion. A sudden change of voice to a much lighter and more playful tone often achieves this. Or moving into another room. Or engaging your child in something that you know will interest him.

Let your child experience the consequences of his behaviour.
If your discipline is going to work, you need to have sanctions that you can use occasionally. In families with more than one child it is particularly important that these are administered fairly, as children are natural champions of their siblings.

Remember that children are responsible for their own behaviour, and parents are responsible for teaching them how to behave.

There is one intriguing paradox at the heart of discipline: the more you forbid something, the more exciting it becomes. You may want to bear this in mind and do your best not to over-react when you really want to impose a particular rule. For example, banning all guns from the house – an understandable reaction to the violent world we live in – can actually make them more attractive to children.

Troubleshooting

Here is a selection of specific issues that you might encounter at different times during your children's development.

Our stepchildren do not get on with each other.

Don't forget that even children who share the same biological parents don't necessarily get on, but they still have to learn to cooperate within the family context. It is not so very different for warring stepsiblings. They may well feel more justified in getting at each other because they have had no choice in the matter and aren't blood relations.

Avoid trying to control what they feel, but do make it clear that some behaviours are unacceptable. Try to be sensitive to their feelings and the fact that they have ended up with stepsiblings because of *your* choices, not theirs. There is no reason why they should automatically like each other. Make sure that certain possessions, spaces, activities and times with you remain special and don't have to be shared.

I am worried that my child is being bullied at school.

Bullying is worryingly common, with two-thirds of primary school children reporting having been bullied at some point. The long-term effects on a child's self-esteem and confidence can be profound, so take action quickly if you suspect your child is being victimized.

Give your child the opportunity to talk to you first, emphasizing that you appreciate how difficult it can be to talk about these things and that it is a brave step to take. Many children are worried that if you intervene, it will make things worse, so reassure them that you will not do anything about the bullying without consulting them first, and that the situation will be handled sensitively. Having said that, you will almost certainly have to consult the school, and should do so if your suspicions remain, even after an overt denial by your child.

You might like to encourage your child to avoid becoming isolated in the playground and to position herself near a group if none of her friends are around. If the bullying is verbal, encourage her to ignore it as much as possible, respond 'You may think that' and then walk away. Bullies normally give up if they don't get much of a reaction from their victims. While it is obviously fine for your child to do whatever she has to in order to protect herself physically, don't advise her to be the first to attack. Not only might your child get hurt, but you are implicitly teaching her that 'might is right' and that you expect her to fight her battles alone.

Follow the school's advice on how to handle the situation, consult websites and helplines, such as www.bullying.co.uk, and put in extra effort at home to give your child experiences that will enhance self-esteem and foster confidence.

My child has regular tantrums.

Try to work out why your child is behaving in that particular way. Is it designed to get attention, to make you give him what he wants, or a sign of genuine distress in response to certain situations?

Usually the best policy is to ignore tantrums and calmly get on with what you are doing, unless there is a likelihood of your child hurting himself. If the tantrums persist, there may be an underlying problem about which a child psychologist or behavioural therapist could give you helpful advice.

I want to leave my partner, but am worried about the effect this will have on my children.

In an ideal world children prefer their parents to be together, but research suggests that chronic exposure to high levels of conflict in the home is much more damaging for them than divorce or separation.

Your decision to leave is going to have significant implications for your children and should not be undertaken lightly. However, if the problems in your current relationship genuinely cannot be solved, it will almost certainly be better for your children in the longer term to have happy parents living apart than miserable ones who have decided to stay together for their sake.

Don't be naive about the potential difficulty your children may have in adjusting to a separation or divorce, and make sure that you remain as consistent as possible throughout the changes. Try to be understanding about their reactions and let your children know that they can talk about their feelings without having to protect you.

Moving on

As the old Chinese proverb has it, 'Govern a family as you would cook a small fish – very gently.'

We have now explored much of what may help you to create the conditions for happy family life, except for two things – the organization of your home, and your own needs as an adult. The last two chapters are devoted to these topics.

CHAPTER **7** The Place
Called Home

*A house without books is like a room without windows.
No man has a right to bring up his children without
surrounding them with books, if he has the means to
buy them.*

Horace Mann, educationist (1796–1859)

How do you react to the quotation above? Is it too harsh? Does it suggest
a certain class attitude? Perhaps it seems a bit dated because of the word
'man' rather than 'person'.

In fact, the speaker was one of the founders of the American public
school system, so you would be right to deduce that his sentiment was not
voiced recently. I have included it because it shows that where books might
once have been perceived as luxury items and implied certain cultural
values, today they are accessible to everyone – to buy or to borrow from
the local library. And, despite the spread of computers, books retain an
important role in our life.

What you do in your own home really matters for you and your family.
The following questions will help you to establish what you care about.

- How do you feel about your home?
- What are its advantages for you as adults?
- What are its advantages as a space to bring up children? And what
  about the disadvantages?
- What have you done to make it more interesting for your
  children?
- Would you consider educating your children at home?
- Are there plenty of books in your home?
- Is your home an appropriate learning environment for children to
  grow up in?

166

Environment matters. And your home is one of the most important places to any family. Most of us can tell instantly if a home is warming or in some way unsatisfactory. Given the amount of time you spend at home, it is hardly surprising that it should have a major impact on your happiness and the life chances of your children.

The home somehow becomes an extension of your personality. In its rooms are the things that matter to you – neatly arranged or scattered about. No one can tell you what to do within its four walls; it is, as it were, your castle. Little wonder, then, that moving home can be such a stressful experience for you and your children.

The home has two components, one physical, the other emotional. The first is created by the building and its surroundings – the neighbourhood, the view, the presence or absence of a garden, the noise levels, the colour and shape of the rooms. The second is influenced by the people who live in the home – their values, approach to life and the way they choose to organize and use it.

Some homes are spotless and would make some adults and many children unhappy. Some homes are messy and would make many adults and some children unhappy. Some homes are clearly designed for the adults to use, and the fact that children are there is a temporary inconvenience lasting for eighteen years or so. In others it is difficult to see where the adults might go to relax, so dominated are they by children's toys and paraphernalia.

In developmental terms, the home is important both as a secure base and a stimulating environment for growth and discovery. In this chapter we will explore the ways in which you can ensure that your home fulfils both of these requirements.

Whatever you think about society at large, your home is a place of safety where you can create your own little world, a place in which your values are uppermost. This encompasses everything from the way spaces are used to the choice of TV programmes you watch, from the kind of food you keep in your fridge to the way you dispose of household rubbish.

Of course, your home is also part of society. Indeed, it is a place where connections are made to the outside world. As a parent you have to think through how you and your children's friends are integrated into the life of your home. You have to consider how your home life will relate to your child's school life.

The home as school

In the UK and in many other countries across the world there has been a phenomenal growth in home schooling over the past decade. Research conducted by Durham University currently puts the number of home-educated children at 150,000 (that's 1 per cent of 5–16s), and predicts that at present growth rates it will reach 3 per cent within the next decade. Is home-schooling something that you want to consider? Visit www.education-otherwise.org to find out more.

Whether you choose to educate your children entirely at home or not, the fact remains that parents are a child's first and most influential teachers, and the home offers wonderful opportunities for family learning. Whereas a school environment has to be pretty regulated, with lesson times strictly observed, a home has no such boundaries. Geography could be a local walk, or involve studying the small print on tins of food to see where it comes from. The driving force for everything is your child's curiosity.

Another important element of learning in the home is that it can be experiential – namely, based on trying things out at first hand. This might involve learning about volume by playing with water in the bath, or finding out about pollination in the garden. The important thing is to experience things rather than read or be told about them. This approach allows you to provide challenging opportunities within a safe environment.

The locality and neighbours also have an impact on you and your family. Having access to the amenities you need, a certain level of privacy and comfortable relations with your neighbours are all essential to feeling good about where you live. You can do a lot within your own four walls, but if you are deeply unsatisfied with the overall environment, this may well affect your ability to create a happy family home.

Five principles of a happy home

Our consumer society encourages us to think that our houses and the standard of décor and furnishings communicate something crucial about who we are. Wanting to live in a comfortable, well-presented home is one thing, but it can become an all-consuming obsession. Some families cease to have any quality of family life because so much time and energy are spent shopping or tackling DIY activities. But a home is more than bricks and mortar. Whether it is big or small, urban or rural, it is possible to make it a happier place for all the family if you follow five basic principles.

Principle 1: Establish clear rules

You have already explored the importance of establishing rules in Chapters 5 and 6. They allow you to function effectively as a parent, and your child to work out what you think is important. Without clear rules, it is difficult for a family to get the best out of the place called home.

In your home it is essential that each member of your family feels that individual rights and feelings are protected. But there are many other issues that need considering too. For example, how can you make sure that the common resources – the contents of the fridge, the space in the living room, the television and so forth – are shared fairly? Who decides when it is OK to have friends around? How much noise is acceptable? Who decides whose music gets played when and where? Who does the chores so that there are enough clean ironed clothes for people to wear in the morning, and something in the cupboard to be served for breakfast?

Where do you keep things? If you were to store shoes in the fridge and have beds out in the garden, you would be living in a state of chaos where it would be difficult to function effectively. For the home to run smoothly there has to be a certain level of organization. But how much organization does there have to be? There is a huge spectrum in our attitude towards mess. What one person considers 'creative chaos' another finds highly stressful. As a general rule, imposing a basic level of organization is worthwhile. Knowing where to find things, having consistent places for bills, documents and so forth takes some of the stress out of family life and means that you can get on with the important stuff.

Sorting out your physical environment is one means of empowering yourself and making yourself less vulnerable to negative or even depressive feelings. If you know where things are, you are bound to reduce the number of times when someone gets upset because they cannot find something important. If your home environment becomes too disordered, you can easily begin to feel that your life is out of control.

What are the rules of your home?

▷ Sit down with your partner (and children, if they are old enough) and make a list of all the rules in your home. Focus particularly on what affects you at home (for example, 'Always wait for everyone to finish eating before you ask to leave the table'), rather than on more general things (such as, 'Always drive on the left-hand side of the road').

▷ Take a broad view of what makes a rule so that you can include all the expectations that currently exist in your family. For example, if you have a dog, perhaps one of you always takes it for a walk or feeds it. While this is not a rule as such, it is likely that family members will see it as a pattern of predictable behaviour ('Dad always takes the dog out last thing at night for a walk').

Or perhaps your morning routine also depends very heavily on one person ('Mum always gets the breakfast, while Dad looks after my little brother'). While some of these activities are more like chores than rules, add them to the list anyway. This might prove useful later.

▶ Think through everything you do during an average week, starting off by working through a typical day. Then look at it through the eyes of each member of your family to see if this stimulates any thoughts. See if you can stand outside yourself and get an overview of what is happening – the assumptions and rules that govern your current life at home.

Sharing the chores

Who does what in your household? Here is a light-hearted way of checking out how much you know about the other people you are close to.

Quiz for couples

Answer the following ten questions separately from your partner, then compare your answers. See how many you agree on!

1. How did you first meet?
2. What was the precise date of your first meeting (month and year)?
3. How many serious relationships did your partner have before meeting you?
4. Which of you is tidier than the other?
5. Who manages the household finances?
6. Who does most of the household chores?
7. Who gets home first from work?
8. How many times in a typical month do you go out together?
9. Who would your partner turn to (other than you) for personal or confidential advice?
10. Who manages the money matters in your relationship?

How did you get on?

9+	You really know each other well.
6–8	You have a good knowledge of each other.
3–5	Who is this person you are living with?
2 or less	You may soon become strangers!

You may be wondering why I have diverted you away from the important matter of chores. Well, I haven't really because the most important thing about chores is that both partners need to know what matters to the other person. For if you are going to be happy, what you actually do matters much less than whether you think it is fair. Knowing what your partner thinks is therefore important if you are to be sure that something you are proposing is going to work for them.

Now let's think about the chores themselves. Have you ever stopped to think how long you actually spend in your home in a typical week?

> There are 168 hours in a week (7 x 24).
> If you go out to work, this might take up, say, 50 hours
>   (5 x 8 plus 5 x 2 for travel).
> That leaves 118 hours, of which 56 are taken up by sleep (7 x 8).
> This means that in a typical week you could spend 62 hours at
>   home but not asleep (118 – 56 = 62).

The daily routines in your life take a lot longer than you think. It is not difficult, for example, to spend at least 21 hours a week (7 x 3) preparing and eating meals. Even cleaning your teeth could account for an hour a week (14 x 5 minutes). Before you know it, days and weeks have slipped away and you have not done half the things you wanted to do.

Maybe the mathematics of a typical week also remind you of the importance of being realistic about what you can achieve. You need to be reasonable in your expectations, or someone is going to become frustrated and demotivated.

What this information shows is that how you organize your time at home and, in particular, who does the many chores that have to be done to keep the house running smoothly need to be worked out carefully. For everyone to feel happy, they should all feel that no one is shouldering an unreasonable burden.

Some parents find it helpful to make a simple chart of who is supposed to do what. This can perhaps be displayed in the kitchen on the fridge door, or stuck inside a cupboard door out of sight if preferred. Others find charts too controlling and prefer to operate on a daily system of trust and questioning to check that tasks have been done. Those who adopt the chart approach often list just the names of the children and their assigned chores, but you can make it feel much fairer if some of the adults' responsibilities are included too. It may also be a way of ensuring that both partners are happy with the division of labour.

Whatever your approach, it may be helpful to work out who does what at the moment and to check that you feel OK about it.

Who does the chores?

Here's a list of some common chores to help you work out who should be responsible for what.

- Cleaning each of the different rooms in the home
- Planning meals
- Cooking
- Shopping for food
- Shopping for clothes
- Shopping for domestic stuff
- Setting the table
- Clearing the table
- Washing the dishes
- Ironing
- Cleaning the car
- Getting the car serviced
- Putting petrol in the car
- Paying the bills
- Sorting out savings
- Recycling
- Putting the bins out
- Making the beds
- Changing bedlinen
- Repairing things

- DIY
- Sewing
- Gardening
- Cutting the lawn
- Buying presents
- Getting the children up
- Bathing the children
- Reading to the children
- Putting the children to bed
- Dealing with schools
- Taking the children to school
- Helping with homework
- Sorting out childcare
- Discipline
- Organizing parties
- Meeting other family members
- Looking after older relatives
- Planning weekends
- Organizing family holidays

Once you start reading even this cursory list of all the chores that have to be done, you realize two things. The first is why you need to get organized, and the second is that it's amazing you have any time left for yourself at all.

Principle 2: Encourage play

If this chapter has been sounding a bit serious so far, read on because even more important than chores is that you, your partner and your children enjoy playing together. While your home needs to be a safe space, both physically and emotionally, it is also a vital environment for encouraging exploration, discovery and risk-taking.

There are seven good reasons why you may want to make your home a place where play is encouraged. It helps children to:

- Learn how to take risks
- Develop their imagination
- Discover about the world
- Develop social skills
- Develop physical skills
- Deal with their emotions

And it helps adults to:

- Stay sane and keep your sense of humour intact, whether you have children or not.

All work and no play, as the proverb has it, makes Jack (or Jill) a dull person.

Taking risks

Go into a public park these days and, assuming that you can find a play area, you are likely to see a small sign warning of the risks of playing on swings and climbing frames. Some schools have stopped installing ponds for fear that children will drown in them. Toddlers' drinking cups have become beakers with lids from which no drop of liquid can escape. And almost every toy you can buy will have a manufacturer's warning about the age at which it can be used safely.

We have, in short, become obsessed about safety. While it is true that far too many avoidable accidents happen in the home, the number is broadly the same as it was a generation ago. However, prominent media coverage of accidents and the growing number of lawyers encouraging us to take action for every mishap mean that many people perceive the world to be a dangerous place.

The consequence is that some children have effectively had all opportunities to experience risk removed from them. They have few chances to work out for themselves what to do in certain situations because, for example, the play equipment they meet is not challenging enough, they don't encounter ponds sufficiently often, they don't experience the effect of gravity on the liquid in their toddler beaker, and toys have been designed to be so safe that they are not stimulating enough.

At home you can invent your own universe in which it is fine to take risks. You can have rough-and-tumble with your children, allowing them to experience the surge of adrenalin that such activity can produce, but stopping when it hurts or they get overexcited. You can let them climb trees that take them a long way off the ground if you have calculated that they have the level of strength required.

Of course, there are some risks that it is simply unacceptable for parents to allow, such as the danger posed by unprotected staircases or unguarded fires. And you will need to agree sensible ways of crossing roads safely. Your job as a parent is not to shield your children from all risks, but to help them learn the kind of protective habits that are necessary for all of us.

More controversially, I would add that there are some risks right in front of our noses where we might want to operate the precautionary principle. I am thinking of the potential danger to health from mobile telephones (including the one you possibly leave on, even though it is close to your young child) and the danger to a child's delicately poised sense of morality posed by some violent computer games. (We know that prolonged exposure to these makes children more aggressive, but they also increase manual dexterity and improve thinking speed, so I accept that you might argue against me on the basis of balancing risk.)

Developing imagination

It's easy for an eight-month-old child to hide. She just covers her face with a tea-towel and, because she cannot see you, she thinks that you cannot see her. As for toys, as soon as they are out of sight, she forgets their existence. Now try these activities with a one-year-old and you'll notice a difference. Hiding behind something has become a great game and one in which the child can probably now cover herself and remove the cover. The relationship with the toy has also become quite different. She is much more likely to remember that you have taken it, and now that she has begun to discover the idea of cause and effect, is likely to see you as the cause of its removal.

At one year old, your child may be seen chattering into a toy phone, but she's more likely to be imitating an adult she has seen doing this than 'talking'. However, by two years of age she may have begun to have long pretend conversations.

Hiding and role play are just two examples, drawn from many hundreds, of the early child imagination at work. In this powerful world of make-believe, old cardboard boxes become castles, dolly is a real person who needs to be fed and changed, monsters really exist, and a long piece of Lego can become either a weapon of destruction or the roof of a house.

A child may rehearse likely or unlikely situations during play. A parent returning from work may have to accept that the carpet has become the surface of Mars or the sofa has turned into a supermarket. Or before school has become a reality you might find your child being the teacher with her dollies and telling them what to do.

The more children are encouraged to create, control and direct their own version of reality in your home, the better.

Discovering the world

Play is the main way in which children learn about the world. Toddlers imitate their parents' activities, such as cleaning up with a brush, talking on the telephone, eating with a knife and fork, and copying the things they say. Indeed, every word you say as an adult is being listened to, ready to be used when the time is right and the child has somehow worked out how it functions.

In the early years children are constantly exploring things. Each new object is tasted, prodded and explored until its inner workings are established. A wonderful driving force of curiosity means that as well as asking countless questions, children are always playing with things to establish what they do. During play like this the child is learning about the world around him by experiencing it at first hand.

Children play at being everything from teachers to nurses, police officers to parents. They imagine what it might be like, then act it out, sometimes with other children, sometimes in a private world of their own. You can help by sometimes joining in and keeping the make-believe going, and sometimes by staying out of it, especially when your child seems to be rapt with his creation and adult intrusion would break the 'spell'. (I am afraid there is no way of determining this, other than trial and error.)

Some family games (such as charades) and many activities (drawing, painting, making music, writing and reading) are excellent ways in which parents can encourage the development of their child's imagination.

Developing social skills

Once children really begin to master language, normally somewhere between one and a half and two and half years old, you can see a huge change in their play. They begin to use words as they act out their creations, often giving a running commentary as they go.

As two-year-olds, they enjoy playing alongside other children, but only those they know very well, such as siblings. Within another year or so they begin to develop whole scripts in their play, and can cooperate with other children to create pretend families.

Play becomes a key way for children to learn how to get along with each other. They learn to stick up for what they want, but also to be flexible and give in so that they can keep the game going.

Play continues to be important for children once they go to school. It teaches them not only how to follow rules, but also how to make them and how to change them. It helps them find out about competition, what they are good at and what they really enjoy. It also allows them to find out more about their identity as individuals.

All the while that children are playing, they are learning essential social skills – how to stay calm (when things seem to be going against them), how to listen (so that they don't miss out on the rules of a game), how to show interest in other people (so that they want them to be in their gang), how to cooperate with other people with different interests and backgrounds (so that they can be included in new activities).

As a parent, you can encourage the playing of various family games because these provide opportunities for children to practise all kinds of social skills in the safe environment of the home.

Developing physical skills

In the very early years you have to barricade parts of your home to stop children clambering on to things that they will either damage or fall off. But as they grow older, passivity often seems to set in, partly as a result of time spent in front of computer and television screens. One way to avoid this is to encourage energetic physical activity.

If you have space outside, you can provide a climbing frame or trampoline. If not, take your children to the park or out on walks where they will find good climbing trees. Encourage jumping games and all kinds of ball games. Your local leisure centre can also provide hours of energetic fun.

Playing out emotions

On pages 52–64 we looked at the importance of understanding emotions. Play is an excellent way of learning to deal with them because they can be explored while not actually being fully experienced. During games, children can experience fear (being caught in hide and seek), joy (the excitement of winning), and distress (the misery of not being included by others in an activity). While the emotions may seem real enough, they are temporary and in most cases vanish once the context of the play changes. By experiencing these emotions and learning that they can deal with them, children become stronger and more resilient.

Staying sane

Being playful matters for adults too. In some ways our culture seems to squeeze play out of our busy adult life as we grow older. Perhaps this is why we become less curious. By having fun we can forget ourselves, relax and maintain a sense of perspective.

It seems that being playful may also have a scientific value to us. Researcher Ellen Langer famously asked two groups to undertake the same task of sorting some *Far Side* cartoons into different categories. One group was told that it was a job of work and that they should get on with it quickly, while the other was told that it was a fun activity, a chance to play. Guess which group did it better and enjoyed it more? The second, of course.

In the busy world of being a parent, having a bit of fun could produce similar benefits for you. Encouraging play in your life and in the life of your developing child is largely a matter of mindset, of giving those around you time to explore and work things out for themselves. If you are constantly irritated by your child's apparent refusal to take something seriously, for example, your sense of frustration is likely to transmit itself to your child, who will become even more frivolous.

Of course, there are times when the playing must stop. Your child has to go to bed. You all need to leave the house. You need some quiet after a day when your child and his friends have been careering around your home pretending to be animals.

But in general the likelihood is that as your children grow up, you may have to work hard to ensure that more (not fewer) opportunities for cooperative play are created in and around your home. For example, you could introduce mind games, such as the word puzzles you get in newspapers, for the whole family to solve over supper.

Principle 3: Develop different zones

The idea of multiple intelligences (see page 150) suggests we all have many areas of talent that, when taken together, describe how clever we are. Whether you agree with this or not, the principle is a helpful one when it comes to thinking about the way you organize the different spaces in your home.

How is your home organized?

Take a moment to think about your home.

▶ How do you use it?

▶ Who uses which bits of it?

▶ Does your child have somewhere that he can use largely as he thinks fit?

▶ Does your home work as a space for all members of the family?

If parents are children's first and most important teachers, the home is the first and most important classroom. It is, in short, a wonderful arena for family learning of all kinds. Of course, it is also an adult living space, and adults do not necessarily want to wade through mountains of toys or trip over pots of paint that have been left out by their young owner.

The simplest way of dealing with this is to create zones in your home, however large or small, so that everyone can peacefully coexist and each area is used in ways for which it is most suitable. You could approach this task by thinking about your home in broad terms. Is it:

▶ Quiet or noisy?

▶ Messy or clean?

▶ Adult- or child-centred?

▶ For use by everyone or mainly by one person?

Then you could look at the various rooms you have and think what might work well in it. For example, if you have a kitchen with a large table or work surface in it, perhaps you could be cooking while your child is drawing or painting. If you (or your partner) need a quiet space for work or study, set aside at least a corner of a room where this can happen and where children are not allowed. In these days of laptop computers this can normally be achieved even if you do not have much space.

Zone your home

One way of opening your eyes to the huge potential for learning presented by your home is to undertake a mini-survey of it as a family. This activity in itself can be fun.

You could start by making a simple plan of your home, like the typical three-bedroom house shown below. Then have a family discussion about the different things you could do in each room. Here are some ideas to get you going:

- Cooking in the kitchen.
- Learning about plants in the garden.
- Exploring maps on the wall of the cupboard under the stairs.
- Reading books in the bedroom.
- Doing scientific experiments in the bathroom.

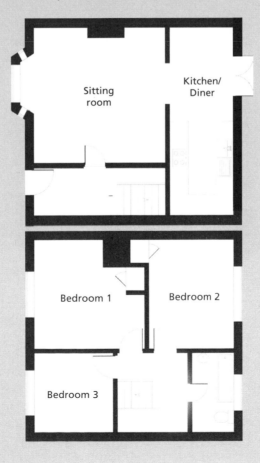

Work out who uses each space most. Are there any rooms that don't work at the moment? For example, how do you organize things if a parent wants to do some paperwork in the living room and a child wants to watch television there too?

You might be worried that if you ask your children to be involved in this activity, they will suggest things that are completely unreasonable. But you could well be surprised. Children have a remarkable sense of fair play and are, in my experience, just as likely as adults to come up with creative solutions that will work for everyone.

If possible, give your children some space of their own, especially if they have to share a bedroom with siblings. Part of a cupboard, a table or corner of a room elsewhere in the home will do. Children need privacy just as much as adults. They also need to be encouraged to take responsibility for their immediate environment. You will need to agree rules that apply to these spaces, especially their bedrooms. It is perfectly reasonable to insist on certain levels of cleanliness, but opinions differ as to whether it is helpful to demand tidiness. After a certain age, say nine or ten years old, if you have told a child that her bedroom is her own space, it may be counter-productive to be constantly demanding that she tidies it up. You will have to decide how much it matters to you, or whether you can 'close the door on it'. Certainly, you will want to review the demands you make and the expectations you have as your child grows older. In my view it is important to respect teenagers' autonomy and give them the opportunity to learn for themselves what it feels like to live in a pigsty.

Throughout your home you might like to consider how you use the wall space. It's great to have all sorts of artwork and certificates on display, plus photographs of the family. Pictures of family holidays make wonderful talking points.

Principle 4: Encourage mistakes

If home is somewhere that everyone feels safe, it is the ideal place for you to encourage your family to make mistakes. This might seem like a bizarre suggestion, but I assure you that it is not. My reasoning goes like this.

If you want to make progress, you have to learn new things. If you have never done something before, you are unlikely to get it right first time; you are bound to make some mistakes. When you make a mistake, you learn from it and try to do things differently next time. Therefore it makes sense to cultivate a mindset in which you actively welcome mistakes and develop lots of ways to extract the learning from them. And home is the best place to make mistakes because it is private and safe.

This line of argument is what underpins everything from learning to ride a bicycle to the evolution of our species. For as Charles Darwin put it: 'It is not the strongest of the species that survive, nor the most intelligent, but the ones most responsive to change.' We need to learn how to adapt to the many new circumstances in which we find ourselves. If we do this, we become stronger.

In practical terms, this means developing a relationship with your children that combines trust, the acceptance of making mistakes and the ability to learn by reflecting on things. The kinds of situation in which this might be important include:

- Letting your child cook you a meal with appropriate supervision and not worrying that you might go hungry if it does not quite work out.

- Trusting your child to walk to the shops and buy some things for you, even though he might not get exactly what you want. (This assumes that you have taught your child basic safety precautions, such as never going off with strangers and trusting his own 'warning signs' – racing heart, feelings of uneasiness, butterflies in the tummy. See www.protectivebehaviours.com for more on this.)

- Giving your older child a deadline by which she has to return home, and being firm but reflective with her if she misses it so that she can work out why it happened and avoid it next time.

- Letting your child experience drinking a glass of wine with you when you feel he or she is old enough.

There are limits to this approach, of course. I am certainly not advocating that you sample forbidden drugs, for example, or even some of the legal ones, such as tobacco.

The process that you need to learn, then teach to your children, goes like this:

- Admit your mistakes.
- Don't blame other people or events.
- Ask yourself some questions about what went wrong.
- Make some changes.

The coaching techniques discussed earlier (see pages 122–7) will help you to pass on these techniques to your child. And developing a positive attitude to mistakes will help your child throughout life.

Principle 5: Promote a healthy, active lifestyle

We are turning into a nation of fast food-eating, television-watching, computer game-playing, car-using blobs. Quite soon children will be born without legs and with stomachs that are half the size of their total body. True or false?

There is, unfortunately, more than a grain of truth in this exaggerated view of the current reality. And parents are squarely in the frame for doing something about it.

'But my child will only eat junk food,' I hear you cry. 'All her friends are the same. Healthy food is boring. There's no time to walk...' Unless our generation of parents takes some action to change this state of affairs, I believe that the next generation of human beings born in certain affluent parts of the world is likely to be both unhealthy and unhappy.

The 'voices' in the previous paragraph are all around us, so it will take some real resolve and determination on your part to put the fifth principle of this chapter into practice.

When dealing with health, it is all too easy to get bogged down in competing claims. Is cow's milk good or bad for you? Is it safer to drive your children to school than let them walk? Should you take vitamin supplements or not? The most important thing is to establish the right mindset. If you start from the premise that you are always going to go for the healthy or active option when faced with a dietary or physical choice, and that you will always try to make being healthy and active fun, you are halfway to your goal.

Diet matters

If you were to believe everything you read about diet, you might be forgiven for thinking that if your child drinks enough water and pops enough vitamins, he will become a genius. Sadly, this is not the case, although drinking a sensible amount of water is undoubtedly a good thing, provided you do not drink so much that you dilute the body's vital minerals. And certain vitamins are essential to our health.

Here are three simple ideas to maintain good health:

- Stay hydrated.
- Balance your intake.
- Eat little and often.

Hydration

Your hydration level – the amount of water in your body – influences your ability to do everything. It is now generally agreed that you will function better if you can drink several litres of water a day. There is no definitive research on exactly how much you should consume, but most children, teenagers and adults certainly need more than they currently drink.

Balance

To learn well, the young brain needs to be fed. Glucose (a kind of sugar) is what the brain and body run on, and is therefore essential. It is extracted from carbohydrate, and your brain uses up some 40 per cent of all the carbohydrate you eat.

However, not all carbohydrates are the same. Eating a sugary chocolate snack provides you with instant glucose, but its effects are short-lived because it is highly refined and therefore rapidly processed by the digestive system. To keep going through an extended piece of learning (or a test) requires food that does not contain refined sugars and that releases its energy slowly. Among the foods that do this are grains, beans, potatoes, vegetables, wholegrain bread and nuts. Nowadays there are many snack bars on the market that contain these kinds of ingredient and taste great too.

Ideally, and without prejudice to any religious beliefs you may have, children need to eat a balanced diet of protein (eggs, yoghurt, fish, chicken and pork) and carbohydrates (vegetables, rice and fruit). Most people eat too much sugary food and too much salt, typically in snacks and processed foods. Salty food in turn causes thirst, and all too often this is quenched with sugary drinks rather than water. Many of these drinks contain caffeine, which is a stimulant, producing an effect not unlike the release of cortisol when your adrenal gland is working strongly. Given this, it would be wise to withhold fizzy drinks from your children for as long as possible. They make the brain alert over a short period, but too much caffeine causes dizziness, headaches and difficulty in concentrating. Many drinks enjoyed by children also contain additives, some of which are implicated as causes of hyperactivity. To be on the safe side, choose drinks on which the label states 'contains natural flavourings and preservatives only'. Avoid products that contain lots of E-numbers, especially those in the low 100s.

Even though there has as yet been little definitive research into the benefits of eating organic produce, I believe that, without becoming fanatical about it, choosing organic options makes good sense. If you knew how many chemicals go into factory-farmed chicken and salmon (both of which are far too cheap these days to have any chance of having been produced wholesomely), you would not give them to your children.

Vitamins matter too. The best way to make sure you have enough of them is by eating the foods in which they naturally occur. Recent research suggests that certain nutrients (as specified on page 184) are particularly helpful to the well-being of both children and adults.

Dietary essentials

The vitamins and minerals listed below are nearly all found in fresh fruit and vegetables, although they can also be obtained as supplements. B_{12} is found in meat, fish and dairy products. The current dietary advice for healthy living is to make sure that you eat at least five helpings of fresh fruit and vegetables a day.

Vitamin/mineral	Good for
A	Eyes and skin
B_1 (thiamine)	Concentration and alertness
B_3 (niacin)	State of mind
B_5 (pantothenic acid)	Memory
C	Immune system and repair of body tissues
Calcium	Strong teeth and bones
D	Absorption of minerals
E	Heart and circulation
Folic acid (and B_6/B_{12})	Heart and mental health
Iron	Blood
Magnesium	Nerve and muscle function; energy
Potassium	Blood pressure
Zinc	Cell division and growth

There is also growing evidence that omega-3 fish oil supplements are beneficial to many aspects of child development.

Eat little and often

Regularly eating small amounts of food is sometimes described as 'grazing', and this type of diet works well for many young people. If you eat a big meal, your stomach and digestive system are hungrily consuming oxygenated blood to fuel this process, so there is less available for your brain. This is why you tend to feel sleepy after a big lunch. The important choice here for a parent is what you allow your children to graze on. Having lots of healthy options available from an early age is important, as is limiting crisps and other salty snacks.

One of the simplest ways of encouraging your child to eat healthily is to shop, cook and eat together (starting with breakfast) as much as possible. It really is that simple.

Exercise is essential

Lifestyles have undoubtedly become more sedentary for a number of reasons. Television and computer games are the main culprits, along with the decline of school sport and after-school activities in some areas, and increasing dependency on the motor car.

The number of obese children in the UK has tripled in the last twenty years. Currently, 10 per cent of six-year-olds are obese, rising to 17 per cent of fifteen-year-olds, and there are similar trends among adults too. All sorts of health problems follow from being obese, including diabetes and high blood pressure.

Exercising the body is essential not only to your physical health, ensuring that your heart muscles work well and that your circulation is good, but it is also a key element of emotional well-being. Healthy children tend to be happier. Research suggests that there is a strong link between exercise and mental health; fifteen minutes of aerobic exercise three times a week is as effective as most antidepressants.

As a parent, you can make walking and bicycling fun, and you can deliberately choose to do both rather than taking your car. You can also limit the amount of television you watch and computer screen work that you do (although if, like me, you are writer, this presents real challenges). Where you lead, your children will follow.

Ten tips for good health

Here are some practical suggestions about both diet and exercise that you might like to adopt, or adapt to suit your situation.

1. Teach your children about nutrition. Put up a chart of nutrients in the kitchen (you can find this information on www.nutrition. org.uk) and note down how much sugar, salt and additives there are in your food. (You can do this by reading the labels on packets and tins.)

2. Cook and eat healthy meals together. Don't add any salt or sugar to your food, and don't put salt or sugar on the table.

3. Carry lots of healthy snacks wherever you go, and keep a good supply in your cupboards.

4. Give your children a healthy snack, such as a piece of fruit, before you go shopping so that they are less likely to hassle you for sweets when you are out.

5. Walk together – to the shops, to school, to the library. Make sure you do it at least twice a week. Take the dog out if you have one.

6. Go for family bike rides.

7. Play physical games with your child, such as catching and throwing balls, hide and seek, tag and hopscotch.

8. Let your children see you exercising and making time in your life for sport. Go swimming together every week if possible.

9. Do jobs together in the garden, or go to the park if you don't have access to a garden.

10. Go on family outings that require you to walk a lot. Visits to zoos, farms and woods are ideal.

Troubleshooting

Given the large amount of time we spend at home, problems are bound to arise there. Here are a few suggestions for dealing with some of the most common difficulties.

My child watches too much TV.

If you are worried about the amount of television your child watches, you might like to restrict his access to it, but also offer enjoyable and rewarding alternatives. Children who watch a lot of TV can get out of the habit of using their imagination, and even lose the skills they need to play. You may have to encourage them by example and limit the amount of TV you watch yourself.

My child is too fat.

This is likely to be because you are allowing your child to eat a high-fat, high-sugar diet while not taking enough exercise. If so, she is also developing unhealthy eating habits that will be hard to shift in later life and can result in significant health problems. Conversely, in a world obsessed by slimness, take care not to overreact if your child is just going through a temporary phase of being a little chubbier than previously.

Consult a health visitor, GP or www.nhsdirect.nhs.uk for advice on how to remedy excess weight. Sometimes children develop eating problems as a way of managing emotional problems, so if you are worried that your child is obese, please seek a referral to a specialist who will be able to address the problem effectively.

My child refuses to eat anything but junk food.

If it is not in your cupboard, your child can't eat it – unless she goes off to the supermarket and buys her own food, which is unlikely. Few children will starve themselves, but healthier alternatives may take a bit of getting used to.

Try to expose your children to a range of healthy foods so that they can discover which ones they like, and involve them in the preparation: children are far more likely to eat something they have had a hand in cooking. Let them know what is being served up for tea, place it in front of them and let them decide whether or not they eat it. Don't provide alternatives if they reject what is on offer. And, if possible, stay calm. Getting over-emotional about food just ends up raising everyone's blood pressure.

Our home is too small.

Your home may well be small and present challenges, but this simply means you have to be especially ingenious about the way you use the space. Clever storage solutions may be bought cheaply from furniture stores and can help to maximize the available space. A tidy, uncluttered environment often seems more spacious and more relaxing to be in.

Try to make sure that even if certain rooms have to serve more than one function, there are areas designated for particular activities. And if your children can't have their own rooms, try to give them some private space – perhaps a lockable cupboard – in which they can keep treasured possessions.

If you live in council accommodation and you genuinely need more space for your growing children, don't be hesitant about contacting the local authority and getting yourself put on the appropriate waiting list.

I can't get my child to go to bed.

Bedtime is often a battleground, but take heart: the battle can be won. First, make sure you have a consistent bedtime routine that creates conditions suitable for sleep. A warm bath and some quiet time with a parent before bed often make for a soothing transition to sleep. TV last thing at night can be over-stimulating, as can sugary snacks. If your child still refuses to stay in bed, you simply have to return him calmly as many times as it takes, reminding him that 'night time is for sleeping' but refusing to engage in any other conversation.

If the problem persists, try the door-closing technique, in which you hold the child's bedroom door shut for a minute or two if he gets out of bed. By staying in bed he gets to keep the door open. Repeat this as many times as you need to, increasing the time the door is held closed up to a maximum of five minutes each time.

Getting your child to stay in bed can be a monumental struggle, but most will give in after a few hours of repeating the procedure. Once the habit of staying in bed is established, it tends to be set for life (or at least childhood).

Moving on

Your home is your space, whatever its size or type. As Nobel prize-winner Joseph Brodsky (1940–96) observed, 'No matter under what circumstances you leave it, home does not cease to be home. No matter how you lived there, well or poorly.'

This chapter has touched upon just a few of the things you might choose to do to make your home a happy and fulfilling place for all the family. Now the last chapter is all about you and your needs.

CHAPTER 8 Looking after Yourself

You can search throughout the entire universe for someone who is more deserving of your love and affection than you are yourself, and that person is not to be found anywhere. You yourself, as much as anybody in the entire universe, deserve your love and affection.

Siddhartha Gautama, the Buddha
(c.490–c.410 BC)

And now it's time for you to hold a mirror up to yourself.

- What did you used to spend time on before you became a parent?
- Apart from looking after your children, what else is important to you now?
- How often do you manage to make time to do it?
- How well do you think you are currently looking after yourself?
- What would you like to change?
- What effect has having children had on your relationship and on you?

In this final chapter I want to explore one simple idea – that the more you look after yourself, the better you are able to look after others and the happier you are likely to be.

While this may be a simple concept, it is very hard to put into practice. When you become a parent, you have to start thinking about someone else's needs above yours – namely, those of your newborn child. This makes sense for the continuation of the species, or there would be a lot of uncared-for infants around the place. But after a while a child does not actually need you 24/7, even though it may feel like it. Nonetheless, many parents find it difficult to reclaim time for themselves and focus on their own needs.

It is easy for you to become so involved in your children that you stop making time for your partner or your close friends. You can end up seeing only other mums or dads who are similarly worn out. You can stop doing any of the things that used to make you happy and give you renewed energy.

Remember, it is just as possible to be under stress on account of your parenting role as it is from the most exacting paid employment. And stress, whatever its causes, leads to ill health and unhappiness.

The five phases of parenting

Most people find that there are certain reasonably predictable phases of parenting, and that they broadly align with the different kinds of education your child is likely to receive.

1. The first six months
2. Pre-school
3. Primary school
4. Secondary school
5. The empty nest

It is tempting to suggest that after a frenetic first six months, when everything is new, challenging, exhausting and exciting, and it is difficult to have much of a personal life outside your role as a parent, it all gets easier and you will have much more time for yourself. If only it were that simple! Sure, things do get easier and you become more proficient at all the things explored in Chapter 5. But your children start to stay up later and ask you more complicated things (and are great fun to be around, at least for most of the time). Until the moment when they finally leave home, there will always be things that you could be doing with and for them. That's why it is really important to ensure you make time to look after yourself from the word go, even if this involves only a few snatched minutes of peace initially.

Return to work or not?

Moving from the all-absorbing world of breast- or bottle-feeding your baby back into paid employment can be an especially stressful experience. Not surprisingly, many mothers agonize over whether to stay at home full time or return to their outside job. Roughly one in three mothers currently decides not to return.

If you are a woman reading this book and trying to work out what to do, it is from now that you need to make a real effort to look after yourself.

If you choose to return, you might find that being at work restores some of things that matter to you, but also places greater demands on your time-management skills. If you choose to be at home with your child, especially if friends of yours have decided differently, it may be a good moment to think about all the other things you would like to do for yourself and, however difficult, try to fit some of them into your life.

Five principles for looking after yourself

If you are to be fulfilled and happy, and to share that inner strength with others, you must begin to focus more on your own needs. The principles outlined below tell you how, and the 'power' that results is contagious.

Principle 1: Recognize your needs

Just dealing with your needs as a parent seems like a full-time challenge, let alone fitting in anything for your own needs as an adult. It is hardly surprising that so many parents give up on themselves and decide just to go for survival.

Don't fall into this trap: it will only lead to unhappiness. Start acting positively by doing the following exercise.

> ## *What are your roles?*
>
> ▷ Take a moment to look back at the different roles you play as a parent on pages 102–13.
>
> ▷ Now look back at Chapter 4, where you explored your adult needs for love. How many different roles do you think you have to play as a parent?

You have to be provider, carer, organizer, disciplinarian, consumer, negotiator, cook, cleaner, psychologist, referee... Most people lose count after a bit. And then, as a human being, you need love, respect, warmth, to be valued, to be touched, to be able to explore your spiritual self, to have your sexual appetite satisfied and, above all, to feel good enough about yourself and who you are, and to be able to keep developing as a person.

The first step you need to take is to think back to a time, which may seem a long while ago, when you did not have children. Ask yourself the following questions, getting your partner or a close friend to help you with them and offer suggestions.

- What are you good at?
- What did you enjoy doing most before your child arrived?
- What would you like to get better at?
- What would you like to find out more about?
- What opportunities have you missed so far in your life?
- Is there anything missing in your life at the moment?

Wishlist gap analysis

- Take a pen and sheet of paper and draw three columns, as shown below.

Current situation	Gap	Ideal situation

- In the left-hand column write down the things you currently do, and in the right-hand column write the things you would like to do more of. To help you work out your ideal situation, it might help to think about your life under the headings: physical, mental, spiritual and social. You'll probably end up with column one containing a long list of all the chores you have to do, and column three listing things such as reading a book, eating out, going to the gym, or having a massage.

- In the middle column note down how you can get from where you are now to where you want to be. Small steps are best. You might, for example, arrange for someone you trust to look after your child one morning a week so that you can go to the gym. Of course, you might want to create a bit of time for yourself just to think through how you can create time for yourself. It is very easy for parenting to be so full-on that by the time you have a moment to think, all you want to do is close your eyes and drift off.

If you are in a relationship, once you have begun to remind yourself about some of your own needs, it is essential that you share these with your partner. For one of the most important and loving things your partner can do is to recognize your needs as an adult and help you to satisfy them. You, in turn, can do the same for him or her. And the more you know about what your partner really wants to make time to do, the more you can step in and offer to do what's necessary so that this can be achieved.

Principle 2: Be selfish

On page 136 you discovered the idea of 'proper selfishness'. Now I want you to take this a stage further.

Take a look at the gap analysis you completed earlier and work out how and when you are going to make your ideal situation come about. Set yourself timescales and be determined.

As Anita Brookner puts it in her novel *Hotel du Lac* (1984): 'You have no idea how promising the world begins to look once you have decided to have it all for yourself. And how much healthier your decisions are once they become entirely selfish.'

There are several other aspects of being selfish, including the following.

Treat yourself with respect

Do you constantly demean yourself? Do you always talk yourself down? Do you use words such as 'fat', 'clumsy', 'ugly' and 'slow' to describe yourself? Are you hypercritical of yourself in public or private? If so, stop it! Only speak to or about yourself with respect. Dwell on your positive points. Be encouraging to yourself. The words you use about yourself matter, even if they are only in your head.

What about your habits? Do you abuse your body by eating the wrong stuff, drinking too much and not taking any exercise? If so, I am afraid this has to change too. What about the way you behave to others? Do you stick up for yourself and for the things you believe in at work and in your community? Doing so is a form of respecting yourself.

If this is all sounding a bit harsh, take it slowly. Monitor the way you are treating yourself over a few days and notice the things you like. Try doing more of these.

Take risks

As the saying goes, it is better to have loved and lost than never to have loved at all. Go for things that you really care about, but remember that much of what you and others worry about is of no significance, so don't fret if what you want to do seems to cause other people concern. Talk it through with your nearest and dearest, sleep on it (many times), then go for it if it still seems right.

Have dreams

What really turns you on? How much of it are you getting right now? Find your passions and be prepared to invest your time in enjoying them. We all need big ideas and vision, or life can easily become humdrum.

Just 'be'

We have psychologist Abraham Maslow to thank for the research evidence that shows how important it is just to 'be'. Whereas many psychologists focus on unwell people, Maslow's views come from his work with ordinary people like you and me. It led him to conclude that we are more likely to find ourselves if we become immersed in what we are doing and go with the flow.

Principle 3: Focus on the five Rs

It's a curious fact that while most people think they can learn how to cook, to speak another language or even to become a better parent, they do not assume that they can learn how to become a better learner and thus develop more as a person. But you can. The good news is that learning is learnable. And you can go on developing as an individual throughout your lifetime.

Most of you will have come to grips with the three Rs – reading, 'riting and 'rithmetic – early in life. While you definitely need these skills to cope with modern life, I believe you also need what I call the five Rs:

- Resourcefulness
- Remembering
- Resilience
- Reflectiveness
- Responsiveness

Unlike the three Rs, the five Rs focus on know-how rather than know-what. Taken together, they provide a kind of curriculum for lifelong learning.

You could think of the five Rs as ways of describing the habits that are likely to make you a more effective learner and develop the full range of your talents. Some habits are more helpful than others.

Resourcefulness means having a good range of techniques at your disposal – rather like having a bagful of suitable tools when you embark on some DIY. Let's take an example from the TV programme *Who Wants to Be a Millionaire*. When contestants do not know the answer to a question, they are given three options: to go 50:50 (choosing between two rather than four possible answers), to ask the audience (doing a straw poll of the people present), or to phone a friend (getting help from a knowledgeable person lined up beforehand).

In fact, these three options are exactly what a resourceful person needs to apply to life. And there are hundreds of other techniques that you might like to learn. Once you feel confident with a good range of these, you can probably work your way out of any situation in which you find yourself.

Resourcefulness is what the psychologist Jean Piaget must have had in mind when he defined intelligence as 'knowing what to do when you don't know what to do'.

Resourcefulness in action

Here are a couple of scenarios that show how you can be resourceful in your life.

Thinking in threes

Take a situation in which you are facing a difficult choice – perhaps deciding whether to work part-time or not. A stark choice like this can be difficult to deal with, so build in a few more options. The question 'Should I work part time or not?' could become 'Should I work part time, stay at home full time, or see if I can negotiate a career break that will guarantee I have a job in a few years' time?'

The more options you can give yourself, the better. If you get into a habit of always giving yourself three or more possible courses of action, you start to see decisions in terms of making choices rather than getting out of impossible dilemmas.

Doing a dry run

This technique is a form of mental rehearsal that can be undertaken when you are faced with having to plan for a new and possibly challenging situation. You simply imagine the scenario from start to finish, viewing it like a film running through your head.

Originally used widely in sports psychology to help athletes get into a winning frame of mind, dry runs are also valuable in more general learning situations where you want to improve your performance. These could be anything from giving a presentation to dealing with your children's bedtimes.

Here are the kind of steps you might go through when doing a dry run. At every stage, think of all your senses and imagine what each one would be sensing.

1. Think of the situation you want to rehearse and the result you want.
2. Ask yourself what state of mind you want to be in for it. How do you want to feel?
3. Imagine you have completed the activity successfully. What sort of words come to mind?
4. Now imagine you are creating a film of yourself in action. Run it through from start to finish, then do it again in fast-forward mode.
5. Focus on the ending. Do you want to win? Do you want to reach a new understanding with someone? Do you want to overcome a personal fear? Think carefully and spend a few moments imagining the ending. What will it feel like?

Remembering, as the word suggests, involves getting the best out of your memory, but is more than just remembering facts. Of far greater importance is your ability to recall ways of doing things and being able to use something you have learnt in one context in other situations.

The more you can transfer what you know from one situation to another, the more you are likely to develop. As Oscar Wilde put it, 'Memory is the diary that we all carry around with us'. The question for most of us is how we can get better at using our 'diaries'.

Consider this example from American psychologists Mary Gick and Keith Holyoak. They gave college students the following problem:

> 'Imagine you are a doctor faced with a patient who has an inoperable stomach tumour. You have at your disposal rays that can destroy human tissue when directed with sufficient intensity. At lower intensity the rays are harmless to healthy tissue, but they do not affect the tumour either. How can you use these rays to destroy the tumour without destroying the surrounding healthy tissue?'

A few of the students found it easy to solve this problem straight away. But 90 per cent of them were able to do so only when they were also given the following passage and told to use the information in it to help them:

'A general wishes to capture a fortress located in the centre of a country. There are many roads radiating outwards from the fortress. All have been mined, so while groups of men can pass over the roads safely, a large force will detonate the mines. A full-scale direct attack is therefore impossible. The general's solution is to divide his army into small groups, send each group to the head of a different road and have the groups converge simultaneously on the fortress.'

The students were able to see the analogy between dividing the troops up into small groups and using a number of small doses of radiation to converge on the same bit of the tumour. In other words, their analysis of the situation got better when the connection between the two sets of information became explicit.

Sometimes we can do better when we see how situations in our work life are very similar to those we face in our private life and vice versa. We can learn to use similar techniques to cope with different situations in which we find ourselves.

Elusive memories

It's happened to us all: the moment something slips out of your mind and you simply can't recall it, no matter how hard you try. It's on the tip of your tongue but you can't spit it out. You walk into a room and forget what you went there for. You stop halfway through a sentence, unable to remember what you wanted to say.

Sometimes retracing your steps to the room that you have just left seems to help. Or deliberately trying not to think about it may bring back the forgotten thought or words. There are lots of excellent books now available to help you improve your memory, especially those written by Tony Buzan (see page 211).

Resilience is a special kind of persistence in learning. It involves being able to deal with all the difficult emotions you experience when things get tough so that you can see things through. Resilient learners have a number of different techniques for achieving this, from 'taking a breather' to 'sleeping on it'.

In a rapidly changing and uncertain world, resilience is one of the most important of the five Rs to cultivate. In his many books about lifelong learning, Professor Guy Claxton invites us to think of developing the 'learning muscles' of the mind just as we would develop the muscles of the body – by putting them through challenging activities. This seems to me to be a really good analogy. If you were trying to shed a few kilos in the gym, for example, you would not sit there with a drink and light up a cigarette. Instead you would get on an exercise machine and sweat it out.

If you want to give your mind a workout, one of the best websites I know is www.themindgym.com and the various books that support it (see page 214).

Reflectiveness is the key to extracting meaning from experience. It involves reliving and processing what you have learnt and asking yourself questions to help you judge how effectively you performed in any situation.

The capacity to reflect is at the heart of what it is to be an effective learner. Indeed, there is a sense in which the difference between living and learning is reflecting. For through reflection you extract meaning from your experiences of life.

A key skill here is the capacity to ask yourself good questions (see page 38 in Chapter 2). This will help you to define any problem you face, to work out why something has gone wrong and to develop your relationships.

Ways to reflect

Keeping a diary can help you to process your experiences and reflect on what is important to you. You might also like to create a 'treasure map' – a collage of images and words built up around a photograph of yourself. The words and images represent things, people and activities that excite you and are important to you. Your map is a work in progress and can evolve over time.

Responsiveness is about putting into practice what you have learnt. Having found out something about yourself or the world, you decide to do things differently in the future. In fact, responsiveness often involves changing the way you behave, and this can be very difficult because long-engrained habits are hard to shift.

To be fully responsive you often have to confront your fears, for you may be dealing with painful experiences that go back a long way. Or you may simply be dealing with difficult parental concerns and weighing up all the courses of action open to you.

How do you deal with fear?

Whether you are dealing with something that happened a long while ago or something that has not yet occurred, the starting point is recognition. You need to give your fear a name and be as clear as you can about what it is. Once you have done this, there are various approaches you might like to try.

▷ Before you start to work on your fear, close your eyes. Think of your favourite places. Think of the times in your life when you have been happiest and most successful. Enjoy them. Feel good about them.

▷ Make a list of all the other times you have faced something similar in the past and found a way of dealing with it. See if this helps you.

▷ Take a look at your fear from another perspective. Imagine you have a ladder. Lean it against an imaginary wall, then climb up and look down on the situation you are afraid of. What do you see? Who is doing what? Could you do anything differently?

▷ Explain your fear to a trusted friend. Ask them for advice. Ask them to suggest some possible ways of overcoming your problem.

If you are interested in exploring any of these ideas, you might like to read other books I have written, such as *Discover Your Hidden Talents* and *Help Your Child to Succeed Toolkit* (see page 212).

Principle 4: Learn to relax

There's a children's book by Jill Murphy called *Five Minutes' Peace* (1986). Without giving away the plot, I can say that the story shows the relief of taking five minutes out from being with your children, and at the same time celebrates the joy of having toddlers. All parents, especially mothers, should read this book. Its title says it all.

But while we all need a few minutes to ourselves on a regular basis, this is no more than putting a sticking plaster on the running sore of being constantly at your children's beck and call and dealing with the other stressful aspects of family life. It does not do anything for your underlying stress levels.

In their famous study conducted in 1967 two doctors, Thomas Holmes and Richard Rahe, developed something called the Social Readjustment Rating Scale to quantify the impact of stress. Their research showed that there is a direct correlation between the total stress people experience within a year and their increased chances of becoming ill. The list of stress-inducing events below is a selection of the things they had in mind because I have chosen only those related to family life. The higher the score (up to a maximum of 100), the greater the stress.

Social Readjustment Rating Scale

Life event	Score
Death of spouse	100
Divorce	73
Separation	65
Death of a close family member	63
Marriage	50
Reconciliation with spouse	45
Change in health of family member	44
Pregnancy	40
Sexual difficulties	39
Addition of a family member	39
Death of a close friend	37
Change in frequency of arguments with spouse	35
Mortgage for loan or major purchase	31
Foreclosure on a mortgage or loan	30
Children leaving home	29
Trouble with in-laws	29
Spouse begins or stops work	26
Starting or ending school	26
Change in living conditions	25

Life event	Score
Change in residence	20
Change in school	20
Change in recreational activities	19
Change in church activities	19
Change in social activities	18
Small mortgage or loan	17
Change in sleeping habits	16
Change in number of family gatherings	15
Change in eating habits	15
Holiday	13
Christmas	12

Looking at this list, it is amazing that anyone survives family life at all. But just knowing that these specific events cause stress helps to explain why, if you are going through a number of them, you may be feeling under pressure.

Seeing the kinds of thing that appear on the list also indicates that, where you have a choice, it makes sense not to knowingly combine too many stressful events at one time.

Types of stress

There is much talk of stress these days, and it is almost universally believed to be a bad thing, something to be avoided. While it is certainly true that prolonged exposure to stress is bad for the mind and ultimately damaging to the body's immune system, short periods of it are not only inevitable, but probably desirable. In the early days of evolution, the ability to fight an attacker or rapidly flee from the scene were critical to human survival. Summoning up a rapid injection of energy via chemicals such as adrenalin and cortisol, our muscles could perform at the limit of their ability for short periods of time until the threat had passed.

In fact, the 'fight or flight' response, as it is sometimes called, is still very much part of the modern brain. When it goes wrong it produces aggressive behaviour, such as road rage. But harnessed well, it helps us through examinations, allows us to excel at challenging intellectual assignments and to endure physical hardship.

201

For the mind to operate at its full potential, it needs to be in a sufficient state of arousal, but not to the point where fear for survival inhibits concentration. It is therefore helpful to think in terms of good and bad stress. The good variety provides you with welcome bursts of energy, while the bad one keeps you at such a fever pitch that you stop being able to perform properly.

How to manage stress

To manage your own stress levels so that you achieve optimum brain performance, think about the following things:

- Which situations tend to make you most stressed?
- Which people make you most stressed?
- What aspects of forthcoming events in your life are likely to be most stressful?

Once you have established this information, there are things that you can do before, during and after each experience to make it more manageable. As a general rule, try to spend the last hour of the day on the least stressful things, such as making some pleasant telephone calls, thinking about the next day or tidying up. If you are out at work, give yourself a few minutes' quiet reflection at the end of the day, and avoid leaving that one last call so that it has to be done in your first minutes back at home. Whenever you feel your stress levels rising, take some slow, deep breaths.

The positive side of managing stress is that there are various ways in which you can learn how to relax, four of which are described below. The more you can be good to yourself, the better.

Do things that make you happy. At the simplest level, giving yourself pleasure helps relieve stress. Watching a film that always makes you laugh, walking in a favourite place, being with someone you really like, making love – all these things produce chemicals in the brain called endorphins, which literally make you feel better.

Take exercise. Going for a jog or a bike ride, working out in the gym or doing whatever physical activity you enjoy is a powerful antidote to stress. The increased blood circulation makes you healthier, and repetitive exercise is especially good at inducing a calmer, more relaxed state.

Take time off. Occasionally, as I have already suggested for children on page 63, you may need to take a 'mental health day', when you make time just for yourself. Use the time to think, potter or relax in whatever way you like to refresh your mind and body.

Meditate. There are lots of books, tapes and DVDs on the subject of meditation, so if you are interested in finding out about this in more detail, visit your local library or bookshop. But if you just want to have a 'taster', try the exercise that follows (taken from *Be Creative*, which I wrote with Guy Claxton – see page 211). It calms the mind by slowing down the breathing and relaxing the muscles.

How to meditate

The aim of this exercise is to help you place your attention on different parts of your body, and consciously feel whatever sensations might be there. While doing this, you should feel relaxed but alert, not sleepy.

Read through the whole exercise before you try to do it. Then, as it's difficult to do something while reading how to do it, make a tape of the instructions, or get a friend to read them out to you. (Choose someone who has a nice soothing voice.)

The instructions should be read slowly, leaving plenty of spaces in between for you to do as instructed and feel your way into your body. The whole process should take about fifteen minutes.

- Sit in a comfortable chair that encourages you to sit fairly upright. (You can lie down, but this can induce the 'relaxed' state without the 'alert', and send you to sleep.)

- Close your eyes and listen to the instructions.

- Take a moment to feel your attention turning inwards. Ask yourself: what is it like to be me right at this moment? How does my body feel? Tense? Tired? Jumpy? Easy? What word comes to mind for your general physical state?

- Now do the same for your emotional state. How are you feeling right now? Expectant? Suspicious? Happy? Find your own word.

- Now do the same thing for your state of mind. What kind of quality does your awareness have at the moment? Alert? Scattered? Dull? Find your own word that seems to capture your current state of mind.

- Take three deep breaths. Breathe in through your nose deeply but comfortably. Don't strain. Then breathe out through your mouth, and as you do so, let your body tilt back just a fraction and make a sigh as though sinking into a lovely hot bath at the end of a hard day. Aaaaahhhh. Do this again... And again... Let your body gently and naturally relax a little. Don't force it.

▶ Now take your attention to your feet. Feel the pressure of the ground. See if you can feel what shape that pressure pad makes on the soles of your feet. Notice any other sensations: temperature... tightness...tingling. Just be aware of whatever's there.

▶ Now let your attention flow up your lower legs to your knees. Notice any feelings in your calves...your shins...your knees.

▶ Now be aware of your thighs. See if you can feel the state of those big muscles. Notice any sensations of pressure or temperature where the seat presses on the back of your legs, or where your hands are resting.

▶ Now let your attention go to your buttocks and pelvis. Just be aware of whatever sensations you find there.

▶ Now be aware of your lower back. Are there any places where you feel aching or tension?

▶ Now let your attention flow up your back into the muscles of your shoulders. See if you are holding your shoulders more stiffly than necessary. Do you notice any other sensations there? See if you can localize them as accurately as possible. Let your shoulders drop a little if they want to.

▶ Now be aware of your arms: the shoulder joints... upper arms... elbows... forearms... wrists... hands... fingers. Feel the sensations in your fingers.

▶ Now take your attention back up into your neck. Again, notice any stiffness or tension.

▶ Let your attention move up the back of your head... over the top of your head... into your forehead... your temples.

▶ Be aware for a moment of any sensations behind your closed eyelids... be aware of your nose... your cheeks... your mouth... your jaw... your chin. See if there's any tension in your face that wants to relax a little. Let your jaw soften.

▶ Now take your attention into your torso, and be aware of your breathing for a few moments... Don't try to change or control it. Just watch your breathing as it is happening naturally right now. Notice where you feel the sensations of expanding and contracting most strongly. Are you breathing from your stomach or your chest? Is your breathing deep or shallow? Fast or slow? Regular or irregular?

▷ Now be aware of your whole body. Feel awareness filling your body like the warm rays of the sun, relaxing and softening you.

▷ Now check out your general state again. Notice if you are feeling any calmer, or quieter, or more relaxed. Be honest. Just report to yourself what you find. How does your body feel? What is your mood now? What is your quality of mind?

▷ If you are feeling a little more relaxed, use one corner of your mind to note what that really feels like in your body...in your feelings...in your state of mind. Feel as if you are making a vivid mental note – as if you are deliberately stamping this impression on your memory – so you will recognize this state when it happens again.

▷ Now see if you can let a word or a phrase bubble up that seems to catch something of this general quality. Peaceful? Relaxed? Quiet? Let your own label come to you. Make a conscious link between this label and the memory of this state so that in future you can use the label as your 'password' to access this state whenever you want. Say to yourself: 'Aaahh...so this is what [your label] feels like'.

▷ In a moment you can open your eyes and come back... See if you can bring that feeling back with you for a few minutes... OK, come back now.

You will find your mind doing different things each time you do this exercise, and, simple though it is, it really repays repeating at regular intervals. Sometimes you will feel drowsy, no matter what posture you adopt. If that happens a lot, try doing the exercise at a different time of day. Experiment with where you can fit it into your schedule, and try to find a regular time when your mind is most amenable to entering the relaxed-alert state. If drowsiness only happens sometimes, don't worry: a good sleep is worth having too. If you can find an alert corner of your mind, use it to watch the drowsy bit. What does drowsy feel like? Where in your body do you experience drowsy most strongly? Try to notice the quality of mind that goes along with drowsy (before you finally drop off). And so on.

You can also try the same tactics if you start to feel very restless, tense or irritated. See if you can find a relaxed-alert part of the mind that is able to observe – in an alert but relaxed fashion – the nature of the irritation. And then, of course, you are equally free to give up – for the moment.

Another common problem that people experience during meditation is that their mind wanders. Instead of being aware of your left knee, you find yourself listening to the sound of the air conditioning, or remembering the holiday you had on the Isle of Wight when you were seven. By the time you 'come to', you find that the instructions are up to the top of your head and you have simply missed the whole bit of your body in between. If this happens, relax. It isn't actually a problem. It happens to everybody (even Zen masters drift off now and again). Just ask your mind politely if it is ready to leave the 'alternative attraction' and come back to the body scan. If it is, welcome back. If it isn't, don't struggle. Just go with whatever is pulling your attention most strongly. (There will be a good reason for it, whether you can see what it is or not.)

Once a state of muscular relaxation has been achieved, it can be really helpful to visualize a personal 'safe place' in as much sensory detail as possible. Safe places can be anywhere, past, present or imaginary, where you can feel relaxed and secure. Some people choose beaches, others caves, or their grandmother's sitting room: it is a question of whatever works for you.

Choose one word that summarizes your state of mind when you picture yourself in this setting. By regularly visualizing your safe place once you have achieved a state of relaxation, and repeating the word, you will gradually create a powerful association.

What this means in practice is that at times of crisis or stress during the day, saying the word or summoning up the image of your safe place will immediately allow your body to discharge stress.

When you have tried out some of the suggested stress-busting techniques for yourself, you could encourage your family and friends to share their own favourite stress-busters and display them on a poster at home. There are many others to choose from, including yoga and massage.

Principle 5: Spend time on what matters

As Pulitzer prize-winning author Annie Dillard once said: 'How we spend our days is, of course, how we spend our lives.' And if you want to be happy, getting your days organized so that you can spend them doing the things that make you happy must be a priority.

As part of this process, you might want to attend more to your spiritual life. This does not necessarily mean going to a place of worship or even believing in God. It could simply start with some exploration – a willingness to listen to the beliefs of your friends who have a particular faith. (Research shows that people who have an active faith live longer and report higher levels of happiness than non-believers.)

There is a classic approach to time management that you could use to get started. Whenever you are faced with uncertainty as to what you should do, use the grid below to help you decide.

Important and urgent	Important but not urgent
Unimportant and urgent	Unimportant and not urgent

Most things in life can be put into one of these categories. Try it yourself.

Six steps to getting your life in order

Over the years I have developed a six-step approach to life planning that really seems to work. Why don't you try it?

Step 1: Make space. Set aside one whole weekend when you and someone special – probably your partner – will not be disturbed by family or friends. My wife and I find that the first weekend back in the 'real world' after the summer holidays works well for us. We are relaxed, and although work is a reality again, it is not an intrusive one. Grandparents or friends can often be persuaded to look after children to ensure that you can have private time.

Plan to do some of the things you most enjoy doing together, and while you are doing them, make lots of time to talk, listen, learn, feel and think. It is really important to invest in this activity. If one of you does not engage, it will not work. Similarly, if your mind is on other important matters, you might struggle to make progress.

Step 2: Get started. You might like to look at some photographs or DVD footage you have taken over the previous year. Perhaps there are some particular items that carry special meaning for you and that you would enjoy exploring together. It's helpful at this stage to give each other private, quiet space so that the initial thoughts and feelings you may be about to share are absolutely your own and not influenced by the other person. You might find it useful to fill in the chart below.

Things I have felt good about this year	Things I have not enjoyed this year

Once you have done this, share the results with your partner. All relationships have their disagreements, so it is very important to avoid any sense of blame at this stage. You are simply stating what things feel like to you. Sometimes you may hurt when you hear what your partner says to you because you will know that you were partly to blame for what happened. In this case, try responding: 'Thanks for telling me that. I hadn't realized you felt so strongly. What could I have done that would have helped more?'

From your list of what you have and haven't enjoyed, you then need to see if you can produce some shared lists.

Things we would like to do more	Things we would like to do less

At this stage you might like to talk about some of the practical things that are important to you, such as careers, income, mortgage and other important practical considerations, but only after you have explored the personal stuff.

Step 3: Agree a common destination. Have you ever stopped to work out where you both want to go in life? This is the moment to do just that. Do you want to be in the same job in ten years' time? What do you want to have achieved in your life? Do you want to work for ever? If one of you is currently looking after the family, what are your longer-term plans?

Take stock of what your destinations have in common. What do you need to get to your dreams? What can you do to support your partner in realizing their goals?

Step 4: Get focused. So what are you going to do together in the coming year? On no account drift into discussing how you are going to do it yet. Start with the big things, the principles, such as spending more time together on weekday evenings, working shorter hours, or spending more time with your closest friends.

Then think about the different areas of your life. See if you can agree one or two things that you are going to do under headings such as: Us together, Family, Friends, Home, Garden, Holidays, Money, Health, Leisure, Spiritual and, of course, Boosting your mind.

Step 5: Do a reality check. This can be one of the most enjoyable parts of getting your life together, as you will realize how much you really *can* take control of. Just hearing yourself saying that you are going to stop doing some things and start doing others is intoxicating stuff.

One of the main skills you may need to develop as a couple is the art of saying 'no' to your partner without giving offence, especially when you are trying to break certain patterns of behaviour.

Step 6: Commit to a plan. It is very important psychologically that you both actively engage in making an agreed record of what you are planning to do. Whether you let your imagination run riot or make very simple resolutions, do commit yourself in words (and possibly even in pictures) to what you are going to do next year.

It is helpful to revisit your plan several times during the year to see how things are going for you.

Troubleshooting

It's all too easy to forget your own needs when you have other people making demands on your time and energy. Below are some suggestions for helping you to look after yourself.

I feel stressed.

Remind yourself that, contrary to popular belief, some level of stress is good for you and that normal life is seldom stress-free. You might like to find activities that bring your stress levels down. For some people physical exercise is a great stress-buster because it releases chemicals in the brain that create a calmer state of mind. Perhaps you could learn to meditate or do a yoga class. Alternatively, potter in the garden or write down the things that are bothering you. A favourite and very simple relaxation is to take a hot bath and listen to some music. The important thing is to find out what works for you.

If your anxiety levels are consistently high, you might need some professional help to bring them down. GPs are very used to dealing with stressed people, and psychologists can often help you to work out why you are feeling stressed, identify lifestyle changes you might need to make, and generate strategies for helping you manage anxious styles of thinking.

I can't seem to make time to do things for myself.

If this is true of you, it is time to sit down and review your priorities. Keep a log of everything you do during the week and work out whether you are really using your time productively. You might feel that you spend all your time running around after other people, but unless you look after yourself, you are going to have fewer resources to help them. Your personal time has to be protected and prioritized. This can be difficult in the midst of hectic family life, so negotiate with your partner and children as to how each of you can set aside some regular time to do the things you want, and create a schedule that you all stick to and respect.

I find it difficult to learn new things.

We all find it hard to change old habits, and new experiences can be daunting. However, the important thing is to respect yourself for having the courage to try something new. Certain skills take time to master, and the chances are that your confidence will increase as you go along.

Find yourself a good teacher or instructor with whom you feel comfortable, and make sure you are learning with people who are at the same ability level as you. Allow yourself to make mistakes and recognize that this is an important and unavoidable part of the learning process. Just because something is hard doesn't mean it isn't worth doing. In fact, the sense of achievement we get from doing the things we find hardest is far greater than from doing those that come to us easily.

Moving on

We have reached the end of our journey together. I hope you have enjoyed it. As I said at the start, there are no maps to guide you through life – only some principles that, if adapted to meet your own circumstances, may help you to achieve happiness in your family life.

Good luck!

Further Reading

Barnes, Gorell, et al, *Growing up in Step Families* (Oxford University Press, Oxford, 1997)

Berne, Eric, *What Do You Say after You Say Hello?* (Corgi Adult, London, 1975)

Biddulph, Steve, *Raising Boys: Why Boys Are Different and How to Help Them to Become Happy and Well-balanced Men* (HarperCollins, London, 2003)

Biddulph, Steve, *The Secret of Happy Children* (HarperCollins, London, 1999)

Biddulph, Steve & Shaaron, *The Secrets of Happy Parents: How to Stay in Love as a Couple and Be True to Yourself* (HarperCollins, London, 2004)

Bradman, Tony, *The Essential Father* (Unwin Health, London, 1985)

Butler, Gillian & Hope, Tony, *Manage Your Mind: The Mental Fitness Guide* (Oxford Paperbacks, Oxford, 1995)

Buzan, Tony, *Use Your Head* (BBC Books, London, 2003)

Byron, Tanya & Baveystock, Sacha, *Little Angels: The Essential Guide to Transforming Your Family Life and Having More Time with Your Children* (BBC Worldwide Learning, London, 2005)

Chalke, Steve, *How to Succeed as a Parent* (Hodder & Stoughton Ltd, London, 1997)

Chapman, Gary, *The Five Love Languages: How to Express Heartfelt Commitment to Your Mate* (Northfield Publishing, Chicago, 1995)

Clare, Sylvia, *Releasing Your Child's Potential: Empower Your Child to Set and Reach Their Own Goals* (How To Books, Oxford, 2000)

Claxton, Guy, *Building Learning Power* (TLO, Bristol, 2002)

Claxton, Guy, *Hare Brain, Tortoise Mind* (Fourth Estate Ltd, London, 1998)

Claxton, Guy, *Wise Up: The Challenge of Lifelong Learning* (Bloomsbury, London, 2000)

Claxton, Guy & Lucas, Bill, *Be Creative: Essential Steps for Life and Work* (BBC Books, London, 2004)

Cleese, John & Skynner, Robin, *Families and How to Survive Them* (Vermilion, London, 1993)

Covey, Stephen, *The Seven Habits of Effective Families* (Simon & Schuster, New York, 1999)

Csikszentmihalyi Mihalyi, *Finding Flow* (Basic Books, New York, 1997)

Davis, William, *Overcoming Anger and Irritability* (Constable & Robinson, London, 2000)

Dryden, Gordon & Vos Jeannette, *The Learning Revolution* (Network Educational Press, Stafford, 2005)

Faber, Adele & Mazlish, Elaine, *How to Talk So Kids Will Listen* (Piccadilly Press, London, 2001)

Fennel, Melanie, *Overcoming Low Self-esteem* (Constable & Robinson, London, 1999)

Gerhardt, Sue, *Why Love Matters: How Affection Shapes a Baby's Brain* (Brunner-Routledge, London, 2004)

Goldenthal, Peter, *Beyond Sibling Rivalry* (Owl Publishing, Markham, Ontario, 2000)

Goleman, Daniel, *Emotional Intelligence* (Bantam Books, London, 2005)

Gordan, Jay, *Good Food Today, Great Kids Tomorrow* (Michael Wiese Film Productions, 1994)

Gottman, John, *The Heart of Parenting: How to Raise an Emotionally Intelligent Child* (Bloomsbury, London, 1997)

Gottman, John & Silver, Nancy, *The Seven Principles for Making Marriage Work* (Orion, London, 2004)

Greenberger, Dennis & Padesky, Christine, *Mind Over Mood: Change How You Feel by Changing the Way You Think* (Guildford Press, London, 1995)

Hargie, Owen & Dickson, David, *Skilled Interpersonal Communication: Research, Theory and Practice* (Routledge, London, 2003)

Harris, Bonnie, *What to Do When Kids Push Your Hot Buttons* (Piatkus Books, London, 2005)

Harris, Judith, *The Nurture Assumption* (Bloomsbury, London, 1999)

Hemery, David, *How to Help Children Find the Champion Within Themselves* (BBC Books, London, 2005)

Herschkowitz, Norbert & Elinore, *A Good Start in Life: Understanding Your Child's Brain and Behaviour from Birth to Age 6* (University of Chicago Press, Chicago, 2005)

Holford, Patrick, *Optimum Nutrition for the Mind* (Piatkus Books, London, 2003)

Honey, Peter & Mumford, Alan, *The Learning Styles Questionnaire* (Peter Honey Publications, Maidenhead, 2000)

Jardine, Cassandra, *How to Be a Better Parent* (Vermillion, London, 2003)

Jeffers, Susan, *Feel the Fear and Do It Anyway* (Rider & Co, London, 1997)

Kaufmann, Gershen, *Stick up for Yourself: Every Kid's Guide to Personal Power and Self-esteem* (Free Spirit publishing Inc., Minneapolis, 1999)

Knasel, Eddy, et al, *Learn for Your Life* (Financial Times Prentice Hall, Harlow, 2000)

Kroeger, Otto & Thuesen, Janet, *Type Talk: The 16 Personality Types That Determine How We Live, Love and Work* (Delta Publishing, New York, 2002)

Lindenfield, Gael, *Confident Teens: How to Raise a Positive, Confident and Happy Teenager* (HarperCollins, London, 2001)

Lister, Pamela, *Married Lust* (Robson Books, London, 2002)

Lucas, Bill, *Discover Your Hidden Talents: The Essential Guide to Lifelong Learning* (Network Educational Press, Stafford, 2005

Lucas, Bill, *Power up Your Mind: Learn Faster, Work Smarter* (Nicholas Brealey Publishing, London, 2001)

Lucas, Bill & Smith, Alistair, *Help Your Child to Succeed* (Network Educational Press, Stafford, 2002)

Lucas, Bill & Smith, Alistair, *Help Your Child to Succeed Toolkit* (Network Educational Press, Stafford, 2003)

Maslow, Abraham, *Toward a Psychology of Being* (John Wiley & Sons Inc, New York, 1998)

Murphy Jill, *Five Minutes' Peace* (Walker Books, London 2001)

Nicholls, Anne, *Is Your Family Driving You Mad? How to Achieve Happier Relationships* (Piatkus Books, London, 2004)

Niven, David, *The 100 Simple Secrets of Happy Families: What Scientists Have Learned and How You Can Use It* (Harper, San Francisco, 2004)

Palamano, Penny, *Yes, Please, Whatever!* (Harper Thorsons, London, 2005)

Payne, Rosemary, *Relaxation Techniques* (Churchill Livingstone, London, 2000)

Peck, M. Scott, *The Road Less Travelled: A New Psychology of Love, Traditional Values and Spiritual Growth* (Rider & Co, London, 2003)

Penn, Helen, *Understanding Early Childhood: Issues and Controversies* (Open University Press, Milton Keynes, 2004)

Pert, Candace, *Molecules of Emotion: Why You Feel the Way You Feel* (Pocket Books, New York, 1999)

Purves, Libby, *How Not to Be a Perfect Mother* (HarperCollins, London, 2004)

Ratey, John, *A User's Guide to the Brain* (Abacus, London, 2003)

Ridden, Sonja, *Help, I'm a Stepmother: How to Care for the Children of the Person You Love* (Metro Books, London, 2003)

Seligman, Martin, *Authentic Happiness* (Nicholas Brealey Publishing, London, 2003)

Seligman, Martin, *Learned Optimism* (Pocket Books, New York, 1998)

Smith, Manuel J., *When I Say No I Feel Guilty* (Bantam Dell Publishing Group, New York, 1985)

Stone, H. & Stone, Z., *Embracing Our Selves: The Voice Dialogue Manual* (Nataraj Publishing, Navato, California, 1993)

Woolfson, Richard, *Why Do Kids Do That? A Practical Guide to Positive Parenting* (Hamlyn, London, 2004)

Useful Addresses

Health, learning and personal safety

www.bill-lucas.com

www.bullying.co.uk – a support site for both children and parents.

www.nhsdirect.nhs.uk – offers a broad range of advice on all aspects of health, including excess weight.

www.protectivebehaviours.com – for advice about children's personal safety.

www.talktofrank.com – information and twenty-four-hour helpline for parents worried about drug abuse.

www.themindgym.com – stimulating exercises to give you a mental workout.

Home-schooling

www.education-otherwise.org – help and advice for parents wishing to educate their children at home.

Making friends

www.friendsreunited.co.uk – for those wishing to re-establish contact with old schoolfriends.

www.people-connection.co.uk – a site that helps to facilitate friendships.

Parenting

www.parentlineplus.org.uk and www.direct.gov.uk/Parents – both contain useful information for parents.

www.singleparents.org.uk – offers a wide range of help targeted specifically at single parents.

Personality

www.authentichappiness.org – psychologist Martin Seligman's website provides accessible approaches to establishing your individual characteristics, including your 'signature strengths'.

www.humanetrics.com – for information about the Myers-Briggs Type Indicator®.

Relationships

www.bcft.co.uk – the Bristol Community Family Trust, which devised the STOP process to reduce negativity.

www.relate.org.uk and www.bbc.co.uk/relationships/couples – for advice about relationships.

Index

Index